MARXISM AND PSYCHOANALYSIS

MARXISM
AND
PSYCHOANALYSIS

by Reuben Osborn

INTRODUCTION BY *John Strachey*

A DELTA BOOK

A DELTA BOOK
Published by Dell Publishing Co., Inc.
750 Third Avenue, New York, N.Y. 10017
Delta ® TM 755118 Dell Publishing Co., Inc.

First Delta Printing

Contents

Contents

Introduction

A comparative study of the doctrines of Marx and Freud has often been demanded by free-lance critics of Marxism. These critics have never shown any inclination to undertake the work, however; nor is this to be regretted, for the only quali-fication for the task which most of them have possessed has been a nicely balanced ignorance of both disciplines.

In the meantime Marxists have tended to dismiss psycho-analytic theory as unworthy of attention. It may be doubted, however, if the founders of Marxism would have adopted this attitude. Friedrich Engels in particular made it his business to pass in review every major scientific development which occurred during his lifetime. It may be that if he could have lived another twenty years he would not have omitted to con-sider the works of Freud. This is not to suggest that Engels would have accepted Freudian theory in its entirety. On the contrary, we can imagine the caustic and ironic sentences with which the greatest of all polemists would have pointed out its one-sided character. But I cannot help believing that Engels would no more have neglected Freud's discoveries in the field of psychology than he neglected the discoveries of Darwin or of Morgan in the fields of biology or anthropology. That old eagle would have swooped upon this new material also, and would have digested it, criticised it, sifted it.

Nor, I am convinced, would Engels have failed to find in Freud's work data which he would have hailed as of the utmost importance for the development of Marxism. For Engels himself used concepts for which the data discovered by Freud were to provide the necessary scientific confirmation. Who, for example, wrote this description of the original form of human society?: 'But mutual tolerance of the grown males, freedom from jealousy, was the first condition for the formation of large and permanent groups.' Is this a quotation from Freud's well-known work, *Totem and Tabu*? On the contrary, it is a quotation from Engels' *The Origin of The Family: Private Property and the State*, published in 1891. Or, again, it was Engels, not Freud, who explained a man's otherwise inexplicable opinions by saying that 'the real motives impelling him remain unknown to him ... hence he imagines false or apparent motives'. And Engels goes on to describe these false and apparent motives for holding particular opinions, not indeed as rationalisations, but as 'an ideology', which had been adopted, not indeed unconsciously, but with 'a false consciousness'.[1]

Can we doubt that anyone who had had the genius to arrive at such conceptions as these would have been profoundly interested when a wealth of scientifically observed data, exactly confirming them, was produced by Freud; when there appeared conclusive evidence to show that the 'mutual tolerance of the grown males' had, in fact, been the key question in the earliest human societies; or when it was shown that it was possible actually to reveal those unknown, real motives which were unconsciously, or 'falsely consciously', impelling men to hold particular opinions?

The relationship of Marxism to psycho-analytic theory is, however, a far bigger question than that of the anticipations, however striking, of Friedrich Engels. Nor is there the least doubt that these sciences are directly opposite. The question is, are they dialectical opposites? Do they, that is to say, by

[1] Engels' letter to Mehring, *Marx-Engels Correspondence*, p. 511 (Martin Lawrence).

means of their very oppositeness, by means of their sharply contradictory character, provide, when taken together, just that unity of opposites in which, Marx and Engels believed, reality can alone be adequately described?

In particular, do the purely empirical findings of the analysts both confirm the main generalisations of Marxism and at the same time supplement and make specific these generalisations in some important respects?

I believe that in this book Mr. Osborn has taken a first step towards showing that they do. He is able to show, for example, that psycho-analysis has, all unknown to itself, provided overwhelming evidence of the validity of the main principles of dialectical materialism. As has often been observed already, the purely empirical findings of the analysts *make* nonsense of, or alternatively *are* nonsense according to, the older, formally logistic, or, as Marx and Engels used to call it, metaphysical, way of thinking.

It is true that the analysts, never having heard of dialectical materialism,[2] continue to accept the metaphysical categories of thought. Hence their inability to deal with the, on their own premises, irrefutable objections to almost every concept of psycho-analysis, put forward by the academic philosophers. The concepts of analysis are, on the basis of formal, un-dialectical logic, flatly self-contradictory. The basic concept of the dynamic unconscious itself, upon which everything else rests, is, from the standpoint of formal logic, nonsense. For, the academic philosophers point out, either a man knows something or he does not: therefore it is nonsense to say, as Freud does, that a man both knows a thing and does not know it: that he knows it and yet is not conscious of it.

Freud has observed, and has now taught us all to observe, the fact that a man often does both know and not know the same thing at the same time; that he knows it unconsciously; that he has the knowledge, and that this knowledge power-

---

[2] This may not be true of the younger German analysts, but it is almost literally true of representative British analysts, and, for that matter, of Freud himself.

fully influences his thoughts and actions, but that he does not
know that he has it. All this is now established by common
observation a hundred times over. It was in order to describe
these facts that Freud had to formulate the concept of the
dynamic unconscious. But what Freud failed to observe was
that in establishing and naming these facts he drove a coach
and four through such first principles of formal logic as that
of the exclusion of contradictions – the principle that a thing
cannot both be and not be. So much the worse for logic,
Freud has implied, with a shrug of his empirical shoulders.
But – and here Freud has shown himself a typical scientist of
his class and generation – he has not seen that once one
logic, one way of thinking, has shattered itself upon the
rocks of observed reality, it is urgently incumbent upon us
to replace it with another. For, unless we do so, we are compelled to go on using the old logic, which no longer fits the
facts, and so to get ourselves into inextricable confusion.
Moreover, before Freud began his work there existed a way
of thinking which fully allowed for just those co-existing,
interpenetrating contradictions which the analysts have found
to abound in the structure of mental reality. In a word,
dialectical materialism provides the only possible rationale
of the findings of psycho-analysis; while these findings, more
especially since they have been independently made, provide
the most striking confirmation yet obtained of the validity of
dialectical materialism.

Mr. Osborn's seventh and eighth chapters show how the
whole of the findings of psycho-analysis are shot through and
through with dialectical concepts. The truth is that the
analysts have suffered M. Jourdain's misfortune: they have
been talking dialectical materialism for years without knowing it. Is it not time that their attention was drawn to this fact
– that the news was broken to them that there exists a method
of thought which makes sense, instead of nonsense, of their
findings; which can find room for every one of their otherwise
paradoxical and inexplicable conclusions?

The dialectical character of psycho-analytic theory is, perhaps, Mr. Osborn's most exciting theoretical discovery.[3] His most important suggestion is contained, however, in his two chapters on the Materialist Conception of History. His conception of the advisability of a shift of emphasis from the study of the character of our environment, to the study of our reactions to that environment is, I believe, of great significance. Mr. Osborn emphasises, in his introductory chapter, the necessity of building upon Marx's great discovery that man's consciousness is determined by his social existence. Scientific politicians, Mr. Osborn suggests, cannot rest supinely upon that discovery. They must not be content till they have discovered *how* in precise detail our social existence conditions our consciousness. For example, Marx predicted that the inevitable development of an objective environment ripe for Socialism would produce a consciousness of the need for Socialism in men's minds. Such an environment has now developed. Has it produced a general consciousness of the need for Socialism? Well, yes, it has, to a certain extent, in certain places, at certain times, and in certain ways. But to what extent, where, when, how? To us, the details, the actual mechanism of the process by which men's social existence determines their consciousness, are of the utmost importance. For upon an adequate knowledge of how this process works our very lives may depend.

Nor did Marx and Engels ever pretend to have investigated the detailed, particular, specific manner in which the interaction of environment and consciousness took place. Engels says this in the letter to Mehring from which I have just quoted:

'We all,' he writes, 'laid, and were bound to lay, the main emphasis at first on the derivation of political, juridical and other ideological notions, and of the actions arising through the medium of these notions, from basic and economic facts.

[3] I cannot forbear to call attention to the beauty and brilliance of Mr. Osborn's suggestion that the dream forms the dialectical opposite of the waking thought process, or of his deduction that this is the explanation of the otherwise inexplicable fact that so much conscious thinking has been undialectical.

But in so doing we neglected the formal side – the way in which these notions come about – for the sake of the content.'

The way in which our notions come about is, however, of vital importance now that the ever-accelerating development of our objective environment is forcing the issue of social change upon us. For our extraordinary notions, our irrational, childish, but formidable notions, bid fair to make the process of social change almost intolerably costly. And the way in which men's notions come about is precisely the subject matter of psycho-analysis.

We shall not be able effectively to influence or direct the process of social change unless we can learn to understand the particular way in which men's consciousness develops from their social existence. For not only psycho-analysis, but common experience, warns us that the way in which our consciousness arises from our social existence is neither simple nor direct. It is, on the contrary, an exceedingly involved, complex, and often baffling process. The psycho-analysts would not claim to have attained to anything like a complete comprehension of it. But they have made definite progress towards such a comprehension; hence their work must not be neglected by anyone who desires to see consciously willed social change.

The principal conclusion to be derived from the study of psycho-analytic theory is, it seems to me, that the emergence of a particular type of consciousness – a particular set of political, religious, scientific, and miscellaneous opinions, a particular ideology, that is to say – must not be conceived of as the passive reflection of a given social environment. It must be conceived of rather as the interaction of the social environment with certain dynamic, subjective urges within man himself. This view, Mr. Osborn is able to show, is fully consonant with the outlook of Marx and Engels. Indeed, they would probably have severely characterised any other as mechanistic and undialectical. But it is a view to which it is not always easy for Marxists in their day-to-day political work to do full justice. It is difficult for the Marxist to avoid attributing almost exclusive importance to environmental

influences, to avoid the tendency to neglect the dynamic, subjective factors.

But, if Marxists have not always been successful in the fight
against a tendency to over-emphasise one factor to the exclusion of its dialectical opposite, psycho-analysts have
scarcely been conscious, even, that such a danger existed.
They have often naively written as if environmental influences did not exist, or, at any rate, could not change; as if
the whole of men's social and economic environment, in particular, could be written off as a constant in the equation of
human behaviour. Moreover we have to try, not merely to
keep a correct balance of emphasis upon the two factors:
what we have to learn is when to emphasise the one and when
to emphasise the other. In the last century, for example,
Marxists were bound, as Engels writes, 'to lay the main
emphasis on the objective, environmental factor in the
determination of political, juridical and other ideological
notions, and of the actions arising through the medium of
these notions'. Today, however, an increased emphasis should,
surely, be laid on the subjective, dynamic factors innate in
men, which the objective, environmental factors interpene-
trate, to make man as we know him? For the environmental
factors are all upon our side already: they cry aloud for social
change. Our business is to see to it that we know how to
interpret that inarticulate cry in such a way that men will
heed it.

All this, no doubt, amounts to little more than the suggestion that Marxists need to be practical politicians, able to
find that correct, psychological approach which will enable
their audiences to grasp and to act upon their message. In
countries like Great Britain and America, which possess a
highly developed political life, there exists a long and rich
tradition as to how men may be most effectively influenced. It
is necessary that Marxists, if they wish to be men of action,
should master this tradition; that they should master the
traditional technique of political activity as practised in their
own country. They must do so, not in order that they them-

selves should become demagogues, but just precisely because it is impossible to leave the formidable weapon of this technique to the demagogues. For in this matter, also, it is a great mistake to give the devil all the good tunes.

But Marxists are scientists. They possess the basic principles of a science capable both of explaining and effecting social change. Hence they must be scientific also upon the question of the detailed technique by which the all-important truths of their science can be brought to the attention of the whole population. Political propaganda, in other words, must be for the Marxist not only an art, but also a science. He must not be content when he has mastered the whole extensive folklore of effective political activity. He must not be satisfied until he has surpassed, and ultimately superseded, this body of traditional, instinctive, only semi-conscious knowledge by a technique of political activity consciously deduced from scientifically established generalisations. Such a new political technique can, however, arise only upon the basis of a genuinely scientific psychology. We shall never know how to influence men, in the sense of enabling them to apprehend the truth more perfectly, until we have a knowledge of the dynamics of mental processes. The psycho-analysts have taken the first difficult steps towards the establishment of such a scientific psychology.

In his final chapter Mr. Osborn makes some suggestions as to the kind of effect which a knowledge of psycho-analytic theory might be expected to have upon Marxists' political work. I think that Mr. Osborn would agree that as yet we must regard such suggestions as stimulating and illustrative rather than as of great practical importance. Psycho-analytic theory is still so incomplete that it is as yet dangerous to attempt to make particular deductions for practice from it. (The psycho-analysts, thereby showing themselves to be genuine and serious scientists, are the first to issue such a warning.) It is certainly true, and will probably long remain true, that those who wish to know how to influence their fellow-men can learn far more from the example and con-

versation of working politicians, from observing Mr. Lloyd
George or Mr. Baldwin, or by imitating, in times of acute
social crisis, the methods of Lenin, than from the most perfect
mastery of psycho-analytic theory. And yet I think that there
is one thing which the study of psycho-analytic theory can
teach us. Acquaintance with psycho-analytic teaching can
help us to exhibit a certain temper of the mind, a certain
attitude to our fellow-men, without which a political cause,
however just and however true it may be, can hardly make its
way. I cannot attempt to define this attitude except by saying
that it appears to me to be well exemplified in Mr. Osborn's
book. His pages are impassioned, and yet dispassionate;
polemical and yet impersonal; acute and yet wise. It may be
that he has best conveyed his essential contribution to the
technique of Socialist propaganda, not in any one thing which
he has said, but in his way of saying everything.

His particular recommendations for political practice may
be questioned. Or, again, he may have made errors, which I
am incompetent to detect, in his exposition of each doctrine.
These will be pointed out, and can be corrected. But they do
not affect Mr. Osborn's essential achievement. That achievement is not, indeed, to have answered the question of the
relationship of Marxism to psycho-analytic theory. That
enormous task will require the sustained efforts of many
thinkers. No, what Mr. Osborn has done is to ask that question; and to ask it in so intelligent, fruitful, and well-
instructed a way that no one who cares for the development
of Marxism as a living science will in future be able to neglect it. And this is no mean achievement. Engels said that
Hegel attempted to present 'the whole natural, historical and
spiritual world as a process. . . . That Hegel did not succeed in
this task is here immaterial. His epoch-making service was
that he propounded it'. Without exaggeration we may say of
Mr. Osborn that, though he has not solved the problem of the
relationship of Marxism to psycho-analysis, his splendid
service is that he had propounded it.

                                              John Strachey

Re-reading this introduction after a quarter of a century, there is less in it that I would desire to modify than I had expected. I wrote then as a Marxist. But I am glad to be reminded that already I was urging that Marxists urgently needed to reconsider and revise their doctrine in the light of major developments in the intellectual field. In this case it was the formidable phenomenon of the emergence of the psycho-analytic theory of the dynamic unconscious which, as it seemed to me, had to be taken into account if Marxism was not to become 'frozen' at the stage of development reached at the end of the Nineteenth Century.

In the event less than no notice was taken by the official Marxists of such demands for flexibility, objectivity and a measure of intellectual modesty. Official Marxism became 'Marxism-Leninism' and then 'Marxism-Leninism-Stalinism'; it became, that is to say, ever more rigid, more sectarian, more 'closed'. There was less and less chance of a re-emphasis of the dynamic and subjective factors which, as Mr. Osborn argues, a study of psycho-analytic theory might have produced.

And now, of course, the officially admitted catastrophe of Stalinism, combined with the capacity for flexibility under the pressure of democracy which Capitalism has exhibited has made the Western intellectual establishment more unwilling than ever seriously to examine such questions as Mr. Osborn raises. I hope that I am wrong, but I fear that it will be some time before the vast and ponderous machine of the Western academic world is willing even to consider Mr. Osborn's whole way of thinking. Nevertheless I remain of the opinion that he has done us a great service, not indeed by solving, but by raising these issues.

John Strachey,
1963

Author's Preface

This book is concerned with presenting a case for the closer study of psycho-analysis by Marxists, of Marxism by psycho-analysts and of both by the general public. It attempts to illustrate the inter-relationships between the subjective life of man, as described by Freud, and the objective world of economic and social processes, whose laws of development Marxism has investigated. Its main argument is that Freudian and Marxist theory constitute opposite, but not conflicting, approaches to the study of human nature; that they complement and enrich one another.

One may express the unity of Freudian and Marxist theory in this way. Both see man as subject to irrational forces that thwart and stunt his life. For the Marxist, these forces belong to the economic and social world, a world that has failed to develop in keeping with the possibilities furnished by technical and scientific advances. For the Freudian, man's irrationality stems from the persistence of infantile modes of thought and feeling into adult life. The irrationalities of the external social world touch off the inner irrationalities of psychological life. The two groups of factors are inextricably bound together, irrational man in irrational society.

The importance of the insights of Freud for Marxists has been doubly underlined by the exposure of the cruelties of the Stalin regime. A movement equipped with the insights of Freudian theory, would have been alive to the dangers of Stalinism; would not have found itself unprepared. In my *Freud and Marx*[1] I stressed the danger of the psychological blindness that made possible the emergence of a Stalin. I now return to the task of persuading Marxists to make psycho-analytical theory an integral part of their outlook.

To non-Marxists and anti-Marxists I would say this. Marxism is the guiding theory of millions of people, inspiring government policy in many countries. To ignore it, or to harbour misconceptions about it, may, if widespread enough, prove fatal for mankind. The threat of nuclear destruction overshadows us all, a destruction that is much more likely to become actual through suspicion and distrust founded on ignorance, than through the malevolent intentions of governments. It would be super-optimistic to suggest that the dissipation of this ignorance would be enough to avert the threat. But it would certainly make some contribution towards a world freed from the shadow of nuclear destruction, in which a peaceful, if wary, co-existence becomes a practical possibility.

The theories of Freud and Marx still dominate our times, stimulating research and thought in many fields of inquiry. Their basic notions have withstood torrents of criticism and attack; and are alive today as ever they were, because they hold important truths for us. In this book, I have tried to present these notions fairly and objectively. I have found it necessary to quote extensively from the works of both Freud and Marx, letting them speak as much as possible for themselves. I do not think that we can begin to understand our modern world without knowing what these two great men have said.

I have re-published John Strachey's original introduction to *Freud and Marx*, to which he has added a note. I wish here

---

[1] Gollancz 1937.

to express my gratitude to him for his helpful comments and
suggestions.

The above lines were written before John Strachey's death.
We all owe him a big debt. His brilliant economic and
political writings will continue, for long, to stimulate new
generations of writers and thinkers. To his memory I dedi-
cate this book.

PART ONE

The Theories of Freud

I

The Structure of the Mind

The basic notion of psycho-analysis is that, underlying all conscious thought and action, are unconscious processes summarised in the phrase *the unconscious mind*. The unconscious mind, for Freud, is more than a descriptive phrase for mental processes not present to consciousness, a kind of storehouse of impressions that have lapsed into unconsciousness with the passage of time. What Freud stressed is the active nature of these unconscious processes, their dynamic quality, influencing and moulding conscious thought and action.

The idea of unconscious mental processes has been subjected to much criticism, especially in philosophical circles. For it seems to involve a contradiction in terms. A mental event, the criticism goes, is by definition a conscious event. Hence there can be no such thing as an unconscious mental event. For this would seem to be to say that there could be non-mental mental events.

The issue seems to be largely verbal, depending upon the usefulness of the identification of *mental* and *consciousness*. Consciousness is a difficult, perhaps impossible, term to define. When we try to do so we find ourselves thrown back on synonyms such as 'awareness', which, in their turn, need defining. It seems that we must accept that we know what it is to be conscious even if we find it hard to say what it is. This was Freud's view; for he wrote: 'What we mean by "conscious", we need not discuss; it is beyond all doubt.'

The 'unconscious', however, he said, refers to 'any mental process the existence of which we are obliged to assume – because, for instance, we infer it in some way from its effects – but of which we are not directly aware'.[1] In other words, there seem to be occurrences in our lives, things we say and do, that point to processes within us with all the qualities of mental life with the exception of consciousness.

Consider, for example, post-hypnotic phenomena. This seems to provide striking evidence of the existence of unconscious mental events.

During a hypnotic state it is suggested to the subject that he should perform an act some time after emerging from the hypnotic condition. He will, when performing the act, appear to have forgotten what took place during hypnosis, yet feel compelled to fulfil the suggestion. He will, for example, open a window at a certain hour. If asked why he opened the window, he may give some such answer as that the room feels stuffy, an answer that suggests that he is unaware of the origin of his action in the suggestion previously made to him. The suggestion has set going a train of mental events culminating in the opening of the window. This effect, as Freud argued, requires the assumption of unconscious mental processes.

More everyday examples of mental events that seem to occur without our awareness are the appearance in consciousness of answers to problems that have defied conscious solution. One may go to sleep with a problem on one's mind, or turn one's thoughts away from the problem and, after a time, the solution appears much as if one had been thinking continuously about the problem except for the presence of consciousness.

Again, slips of the tongue, pen and many similar everyday errors, seem to show an interference with conscious intention consistent with the occurrences of unconscious mental events. Freud gives an amusing example in his *Psychopathology of*

[1] Freud, *New Introductory Lectures* (Hogarth Press 1932), p. 94.

Everyday Life. 'A wealthy but not very generous host invited his friends for an evening dance. Everything went well until about 11.30 p.m. when there was an intermission, presumably for supper. To the great disappointment of most of the guests there was no supper; instead, they were regaled with thin sandwiches and lemonade. As it was close to Election day the conversation centred on the different candidates; and as the discussion grew warmer, one of the guests, an ardent admirer of the Progressive Party candidate, remarked to the host; "You may say what you please about Teddy, but there is one thing – he can always be relied upon; he always gives you a square meal," wishing to say "square deal". The assembled guests burst into a roar of laughter, to the great embarrassment of the speaker and the host, who fully understood each other.'

Modern neurophysiological theory is consistent with the notion of unconscious mental events. If we accept that all mental events depend upon the activity of the brain, the discovery that the cortex, the surface of the brain consisting of millions of nerve cells, is in constant activity, provides a neurological basis for the notion of unconscious mental events. For this cortical activity is not limited to areas that may be involved, at any time, in consciousness and Freud, who had hoped that his theories could find a neurological foundation, would have been intensely interested in the researches of the workers with the electroencephalograph recorder.

Freud distinguished two kinds of unconscious mental life. There are, firstly, those mental processes which, while unconscious are, relatively easily, transformed into consciousness. For these unconscious mental processes, Freud used the term 'pre-conscious'. For example, I may say that I am now conscious of the pressure of pen to paper, the whiteness of the paper, a piano being played in another room. My brother asks me for a telephone number. I pause and with no great effort recall it. I am now conscious of it. In this sense, one might speak of a transformation of unconscious mental content into conscious content. The pre-conscious has become conscious.

But it is not this sense of the unconscious that forms the basic concept of Freudian theory. Freud argued that there are mental events which, only with great difficulty if at all, can be transformed into consciousness. There operates a repressive system, as Freud discovered when attempting to revive childhood memories, which resists any attempt to bring unconscious elements into consciousness. 'The whole of psycho-analytic theory,' Freud wrote, 'is in fact built upon the perception of the resistance exerted by the patient when we try to make him conscious of his unconscious. The objective indication of resistance is that his associations stop short or wander far away from the theme that is being discussed.' Thus a great deal of childhood life said to be 'forgotten', in the sense of having faded with the passage of time, has, in Freud's view, been repressed. We shall discuss later why this repression has occurred.[2] What is important, in Freudian theory, is that, although repressed, these childhood experiences may continue to exert an important influence on everyday thought and action. Repression, Freud suggested, is the psychological equivalent of the process in the body by which a protective wall of tissue isolates a diseased part from the rest of the body.

The earliest formulations that Freud made of the repressive forces likened them to a censor. The mind was pictured as a kind of three-storey dwelling. On the top floor were the respectable members of the conscious family. Below them were the pre-conscious people, quiet, decent folk, who were permitted to visit their neighbours above. True a policeman stood on the stairs between but he was a genial soul, rarely forbidding passage. But the dwellers on the ground floor were a tumultuous, uncultured crowd, noisily clamouring to pass the overworked policeman between them and the pre-conscious folk. Occasionally one slipped by, generally in a disguise that represented him as a harmless person and when

[2] See chapter 2.

night had brought a relaxation of the policeman's vigilance. These policemen were a picturesque representation of the repressive forces.

Freud has often been criticised for using language which seemed to refer to actual entities within the mind, evoking a picture of a strange subterranean world inhabited by queer near-human creatures. Freud wrote before such terms as 'constructs' and 'intervening variables' were part of the language of psychology. But he made it clear that his aim was to present symbolically what are essentially mental activities. His concepts, he claimed, perform an analogous function to the concepts of waves, electrons, energy, used in physical science, linking together otherwise disparate aspects of human knowledge and experience into meaningful patterns. Thus in his *Introductory Lectures*, while acknowledging that his concepts are sometimes 'crude' he defends them on the grounds that, like Ampère's manikin swimming in the electric current, they are useful aids to understanding, 'and, in so far as they do assist comprehension, are not to be despised'.[3]

The division of mental life into conscious, preconscious and unconscious seemed, to Freud, to present too static a picture of the mind. Hence he introduced concepts less suggestive of particular regions of the mind and more suggestive of mental activity.[4]

These are the concepts of the id, ego and super-ego which I propose to describe briefly.

The concept of the id was introduced to refer to those unconscious aspects of mental life which conflict strongly with conscious standards, standards that the individual acquires from family and social life. Freud borrowed the term from Nietzsche because it seemed well suited, as a derivative of the Latin impersonal pronoun, to express this incompatibility with conscious standards. The *id* is the *it*, the something, that sweeps over us when we find ourselves impelled to act con-

---

[3] S. Freud, *Introductory Lectures* (Allen and Unwin 1923), p. 250.

[4] For this reason, too, Freud preferred not to use the term sub-conscious. It was too suggestive of a particular region of the mind and too little of mental activity.

trary to 'good taste' or accepted standards. We tend to refer to such impulses as if they are foreign to our main personality in such phrases as 'it came over me'; 'I couldn't help myself'.

The id refers to the primitive, instinctive demands in man's nature unaffected by moral or social considerations. The characteristics of the id on which Freud placed particular stress are its unconditional demands for satisfaction, its irrationality, its amorality. It comprises the so-called life and death instincts, the inherited racial qualities that link us with the rest of the animal kingdom. Moreover, repressed experiences that have been too painful for conscious life join the stream of id impulses. The id is ruled by the 'pleasure principle', that is, it demands immediate and unconditional satisfaction with no consideration of fitness of time or place.

A human organism that was completely at the mercy of the impulses of the id would very quickly find itself in difficulties, would, indeed, quickly perish. For the external world does not readily grant the satisfaction of our desires. We have to learn to defer this satisfaction until favourable opportunities occur when it can be achieved in safety.

In the very young child, the id is predominant. The child yells for whatever it wants. But gradually it learns that there are barriers to the satisfaction of its wants. Its parents do not always immediately respond. Sometimes, its demands are met with punishment. The painful experience that the world does not yield so readily to its wishes, stimulates a change within the id. A part of the id pays attention to the outer world, becomes aware, or conscious, of it. This modification within the id whereby attention is paid to the external world was termed by Freud, the *ego*. How this transformation of id into ego is effected is not known. It is a necessary postulate of Freudian theory that it takes place and one may assume that the impact of external reality as a limiting factor, triggers off a maturation process which leads to the emergence of conscious, rational qualities of mental life.

The ego, in Freud's view, has the task of restraining the demands of the id, seeking satisfaction for them on a reality level. In other words, it opposes the 'reality principle' to the 'pleasure principle' of the id. It originates within the id chiefly as a means of finding forms of satisfaction for id impulses in the external world. 'On the whole,' wrote Freud, 'the ego has to carry out the intentions of the id; it fulfils its duty if it succeeds in creating the conditions under which these intentions can best be fulfilled. One might compare the relation of the ego to the id with that between a rider and his horse. The horse provides the locomotive energy, and the rider has the prerogative of determining the goal and of guiding the movements of his powerful mount towards it. But all too often in the relations between the ego and the id we find a picture of the less ideal situation in which the rider is obliged to guide his horse in the direction in which it itself wants to go.'[5]

We may sum up the main characteristics of the ego, as seen by Freud, as follows: It mediates between the id and external reality. While its relationship with the id remains on an unconscious level, its relationship to the external world is a conscious one. It is ruled by a reality principle, a principle that takes cognizance of the possibilities presented by the external world as opposed to the pleasure principle of the id. In fulfilling this reality principle its task is also to maintain a censorship of mental processes likely to offend against conscious standards. It gives its contents verbalised form.

The ego, however, is born in the early years of life, when strong emotional bonds between the child and its parents are paramount. The ego of the young child is too weak to deal alone with the imperious demands of the id. It has to strengthen itself with the authority of its parents. The commands and directions of the parents, externally applied to the child, are reproduced within the child's mind as powerful inhibiting factors. A process of identification takes place by which the attitudes of the parents, their standards of behaviour are incorporated into the child's mind. The process is an extremely complicated one, somewhat analogous to that of

[5] *New Introductory Lectures*, p. 103.

imitating the standards of a person one both loves and fears, and occurring on an unconscious level. Freud speaks of this process as one of *introjection*, of internalising, so to say, the authority and influence of the parents (and other adults important in the child's life).

These internalised attitudes of the parents are what Freud calls the *super-ego*. The super-ego is thus a modification of the ego when the ego is too weak to confront the problems and demands both of the id and external reality alone. It is a kind of mental representation of the parents and other adults within the mind, a representation, Freud insists, endowed with the exaggerated qualities which parents appear to have to the child mind, qualities of omniscience, of severity; the qualities, in short, of an unquestionable authority.

The Freudian theory of the super-ego may, at first sight, seem to give a queer view of the development of mental life. The notion of the ego identifying a part of itself with the parents and other adults, modelling itself upon the exaggerated picture of parental authority as it occurs in the child mind, may seem like some fantastic piece of mythology. But what, after all, is it saying? It says that, in some manner not yet fully understood, the influence of the parents and other important adults in the child's life, persists as the child grows and plays a determining part in his adult behaviour. The concept of the super-ego is required to account for the persistence into adult life of childhood standards, the compulsive character of much behaviour that falls far below what rational and humane considerations would expect. One has only to reflect on some of the terrible things that people have sometimes felt impelled to do, from the Nazis who felt an obligation to destroy Jews to those many cruelties in religious and political history performed from a sense of duty. The Freudian theory of the super-ego asks us to accept that many, if not most, adults carry around with them as an integral part of their psychologies, patterns and modes of behaviour which belong to the uncritical stage of their childhoods and which continue to exert a compulsive influence in adult life.

Let us now see in broad outline the kind of picture of mental life presented by Freudian theory. If we ignore the special terminology in which Freudian theory is presented, we get a picture of dynamic interplay between mental life and the external world in which mental life undergoes modification in the process of adaptation to the facts of the external world. What Freud refers to as the ego are qualities of consciousness, of growing detailed awareness of the external reality and a capacity to harmonise inner needs with outer possibilities of satisfaction. That this kind of development in mental life takes place, is, I think, a matter of everyday observation. That children learn to adapt themselves to the demands of external reality, and display a growth of rational qualities, is a fact of human development that needs no emphasis. The Freudian contribution is to point out the extremely complex pattern of development which this involves. If the transition from the irrationalities and dependence of childhood was a simple matter of acquiring rational adult self-dependent qualities there would be no need for psycho-analytic research.

Where Freudian theory opens itself to criticism, I think, is in the kind of relationship it depicts between, broadly speaking, the conscious aspects of mental life and those which are predominantly unconscious. Psycho-analytic theory is sometimes presented as if the ego is exclusively an instrument for serving unconscious aims and is incapable of asserting any independent control over them. In non-Freudian language, it sometimes appears as though Freudian theory asserts that our rational selves are completely dominated by emotional and irrational ends, serving only to find outlets for emotional drives in the external world which do not conflict too openly with currently accepted standards. The growth of rational and conscious qualities of mental life, in this interpretation, involves no qualitative stage in mental growth. The conscious mind is merely an extension of an unconscious substratum, probing for permissible channels for expression of unconscious tendencies.

It is, of course, true that men are much less rational than they like to think themselves, that they do tend to use their conscious qualities in the service of irrational ends.

One has only to reflect how science has so often been used for destruction and death to realise how much reason is the slave of unreason. But the existence of a science of psychology, and psycho-analysis in particular, is an indication that this enslavement is not complete. The slave who is unaware of his slavery, who accepts it as a natural thing, will always be a slave. The first condition of revolt against any form of slavery is the recognition that slavery exists. This is true of the servitude of our rational selves to irrational ends, of the ego to the id. When men realise, as they are beginning to realise, that their rational selves serve irrational ends, they are taking the first steps to end this servitude.

It is worth recording that Freud, while stressing the weakness and dependence of the ego, did not take a wholly pessimistic view of its relation to the id. In one book he rebukes those psycho-analysts who make too much of the weakness of the ego, and stresses its potentialities for psychological control. He writes: 'At this point it is relevant to ask how I can reconcile this acknowledgment of the might of the ego with the description I have given in *The Ego and the Id*. In that book I drew a picture of the dependence upon the id and upon the super-ego which revealed how powerless and apprehensive it was in regard to both and with what an effort it maintained its superiority over them. This view has been widely echoed in psycho-analytic literature. A great deal of stress has been laid on the weakness of the ego in relation to the id and our rational elements in the face of daemonic forces within us; and there is a strong tendency to make what I have said into a foundation of a psycho-analytic Weltanschauung. Yet surely the psycho-analyst, with his knowledge of the way in which repression works, should, of all people, be restrained from adopting such extreme and one-sided views.'[6]

[6] S. Freud, *Inhibitions, Symptoms and Anxiety* (Hogarth 1936), pp. 28-9.

In spite, then, of the pessimistic character of much of
Freud's writings and the tendency for psycho-analytic theory
to present human nature as basically unalterable, there is a
recognition of the qualitative character of ego development.
Writers like Fromm and Horney have been reformulating
analytic theory in more social terms, consistent with the view
that the ego shows qualities not reducible to id impulses.
'The key problem of psychology,' wrote Fromm, 'is that of
the specific kind of relatedness of the individual towards the
world and not that of the satisfaction or frustration of this or
that instinctual need *per se.*'[7] Even such an orthodox psycho-
analyst as Dr. Ernest Jones could write, in 1959, 'It is a tenet
of psycho-analysis that man is throughout a social creature,
and that the attempted distinction between individual and
social psychology is inherently fictitious. By this is meant that
his mind develops entirely out of interactions between him
and other human beings, and that an individual not so built
up is unthinkable.'[8]

The 'specific kind of relatedness' of man to the world is
displayed in his social consciousness, a consciousness of his
relations and responsibilities to others. Unfortunately, this
consciousness is still a weak force in human life, very much
influenced by irrationalities carried over from childhood.
Hence any social and political thinking, as I shall argue later,
must begin with this: the fact that men and women, in many
important aspects of their psychologies, have failed to transcend the habits and modes of thinking of childhood.

[7] E. Fromm, *Man for Himself* (Routledge, 1949).
[8] Ernest Jones, *Free Associations* (Hogarth Press 1959), p. 153.

2

Freud's Sexual Theory

The ego has the difficult task of adapting instinctive impulses to the demands of reality. In this sense, conscious behaviour is the product of interaction between instinctive impulses and an outer reality that tends to restrict and deny them expression.

At this stage it is not my intention to examine the nature of that reality which forms man's environment, but to outline the general theory of instinctive life given by psycho-analysis. If, therefore, the account seems to over-stress the part played by instinctive impulses, it does so necessarily, so that when we do examine the environmental situations in which they express themselves, we shall not tend to minimise their importance.

Definitions of instincts are varied. In general, they are considered to be fundamental innate impulses connected with the preservation of the individual and the species. 'An instinct,' wrote Freud, 'may be described as having a source, an object and an aim. The source is a state of excitation within the body, and its aim is to remove that excitation; in the course of its path from its source to the attainment of its aim the instinct becomes operative mentally. We picture it as a certain sum of energy forcing its way in a certain direction.'[1]

[1] *New Introductory Lectures*, p. 125.

Attempts have been made by psychologists to list the instincts which seemed to Freud to miss the real nature of the instinctive life. He wrote: 'You know how popular thought deals with the instincts. It postulates as many different instincts as may be needed – an instinct of assertiveness, instincts of imitation and play, a social instinct, and a great many more besides. It takes them up, as it were, lets each do its particular work, and then drops them again. We have always suspected that behind this multitude of small occasional instincts there lies something much more serious and powerful, which must be approached with circumspection.'[2]

In attempting to get behind the multiplicity of instinctive responses to their fundamental sources, Freud has been led to formulate two main groups – *Eros*, or life instincts and *Death*, or destructive instincts.

We shall consider this grouping towards the end of this chapter, but for the moment we shall deal with the sexual impulses included in the group of Eros, which, biologically, serve the needs of reproduction.

Freud's views on the sexual instinct aroused violent opposition when first propounded. He could expect nothing else, for since he considers that the repressed material in the unconscious is largely infantile and sexual in character and out of harmony with conscious standards, his very suggestion outraged those standards and evoked strong condemnation in their defence.

By sexual Freud meant 'the energy of those instincts which have to do with all that may be comprised under the word "love". On the one hand, self-love, and, on the other hand, love for parents, children, and love for humanity in general, and also devotion to concrete objects and abstract ideas.'

The meaning he attached to the word is thus enormously wider than popular usage that restricts it to the adult relationship leading to the sexual act, considering the other manifestations described by Freud as due to the working of some other instinct. Dr. McDougall, for example, accounts

[2] *New Introductory Lectures*, p. 124.

for the love which parents have for their children as due to the operation of a 'tender instinct'.

Still further did Freud offend conventional belief when he imputed a sex-life to children from the earliest days of life. He pointed to the possessiveness with which parents of the opposite sex are regarded, the desire to be petted, the blissful expression when taken into the arms, the contented sucking of the thumb with angry cries when dispossessed, the pleasure that children show when bodily stimulated by tickling and so forth as evidence of early sex-life.

In early sex-life, what are known as component sexual instincts dominate. They have a more or less independent existence of each other, with their own modes of seeking gratification. In the course of sexual development they are all integrated, but sometimes a component instinct may dominate the sex-life of the adult, compelling him to seek sexual satisfaction of an infantile character. Perversions are seen, in Freudian theory, as the retention, in adult life, of infantile modes of sexual behaviour.

In his account of the component instincts[3] Freud stresses, in particular, those associated with the oral and anal zones of the body. Thus the activities of sucking and biting present, he says, an early form of sexual gratification. Later workers have developed the notion of oral character traits which are assumed to relate to the way the oral sexual needs of the child were met. The studies of Abraham and Glover, for example, suggest that the experience of oral gratification or frustration, in childhood, leads to the orally gratified or orally ungratified types in later character formation. The former tends to be highly optimistic, generous, sociable, open to new ideas whereas the latter tends to be deeply pessimistic, withdrawn, insecure and passive. The concept of bipolarity in oral character development has been subjected to investigation by Dr. Frieda Goldman-Eisler. She made a factorial study of 115 adults, using rating scales and questionnaires and appears to

[3] Freud, *Three Contributions to the Theory of Sex*, Modern Library, New York 1938.

have identified a bipolar type factor which she claims: 'shows a striking correspondence to psychoanalytic oral character types as described by Abraham, Glover, Jones and Bergler.'[4]

The stimulation of the zone in the neighbourhood of the anus, the anal erotic zone, is the form of gratification sought by another group of component instincts. The attitude of the parents and the child to the act of excretion strongly influences, it is claimed, the later character formation. The child learns that its parents place a value on the performance of this function, and in its ability to please or displease them, a sense of power grows. Its excrement is the first thing a child has to offer the world and its later attitudes to money, people, work, art and life in general, say the psycho-analysts, may be greatly affected by its attitude as an infant, to the process of excretion.

This may seem a far-fetched claim but it must be remembered that practically the whole of the second year of a baby's life is taken up with training by the parents of the child's control of excretion. The child is often exhorted, praised and threatened. It learns to express defiance to its mother by withholding its faeces. In later life, this tendency to withold may be a subjective factor leading to hoarding money, to obstinacy and miserliness, while willingness to perform the excretory function as a means of pleasing its parents, and also because of the organic pleasure derived from the act, may be transformed into generosity, extravagance, or forms of productive activity such as writing, painting and speaking.

As with oral character traits, attempts have been made to validate this Freudian notion of anal character traits. The results are not clearcut but certainly tend to be consistent with Freudian theory.[5]

---

[4] Frieda Goldman Eisler, *Breastfeeding. Personality In Nature, Society and Culture*, Edited by Kluckhohn & Murray, N. York Knopf 1959.

[5] In *The Structure and Origin of the Anal Character* (Genet. Psychol. Monogr., 1957) Halla Belloff reports some interesting results from her investigation. Seventy-five undergraduates answered questionnaires involving 28 items relating to anal character traits. A significant factor closely related to Freudian concept of anal traits was found. We shall discuss, later, the scientific status of Freudian theory and its susceptibility to experimental

The integration of these and other component instincts takes place, in the growing child, under the dominance of impulses associated with the genitals. The well-balanced adult exhibits impulses derived from the component instincts but these merely subserve the purposes of the sexual act. To arrive at that stage the sexual impulses undergo a developmental process which we shall now consider.

There are two main periods in sexual development, separated by a latency period, in which little or no development of the instincts takes place. The first period, according to Freud, is the most important, for it lays down the lines along which the revival of sexual impulses later takes its course. This period is from infancy to five years, and has three main stages in which one of the component instincts plays a dominating part.

The first stage is known as the auto-erotic stage. It occurs in the earliest weeks of childhood, when the child has no awareness of itself as an individual. The various component instincts seek their gratification more or less independently, and the child's sexual life is confined to sensory pleasures derived from stimulating the body. Because of the importance of sucking at this stage, the oral component instinct is the most evident. Towards the second year of his life the child's self-awareness grows. The sexual instinct becomes directed towards the self, as a love object. For this reason, Freud called this stage narcissism, after the character in Greek mythology who fell in love with his own image.

The transition from the auto-erotic to this stage is probably largely helped by the insistence of mothers, who had previously tolerated the child's inability to control its excretions, that the child should be taught to be clean. It gives him a sense of power in which he revels by cruel and boisterous

verification. Here I would only say that, like all anthropological sciences, its predictive value and therefore its testability is low. There are too many variables which escape the rigorous control required in an experimental situation. Freudian theory, we shall see, performs rather a unifying rôle, suggesting how aspects of human experience are inter-related. Nevertheless, research, where this has been possible, has certainly not contradicted the main tenets of Freudian theory.

behaviour, loving to show off his body by running about
naked.

The most critical period in development is the third stage.
The child's interest turns outwards and he seeks for his love
objects in the outer world. It is inevitable that the first object
he looks to are those nearest to it – the members of his own
family. In this situation there occurs what Freud called the
Oedipus complex, so called after the play by Sophocles in
which Oedipus, in fulfilment of a prophecy, unwittingly kills
his own father and marries his own mother. This complex is
described by Freud as follows: 'I refer to that rivalry of
affections in which sexual elements are plainly emphasised.
The son, when quite a little child, already begins to develop a
peculiar tenderness towards his mother, whom he looks upon
as his own property, regarding his father in the light of a rival
who disputes this sole possession of his; similarly the little
daughter sees in her mother someone who disturbs her tender
relation to her father and occupies a place which she feels she
herself could very well fill.' The dreams of many people, said
Freud, 'bring to light the wish for the removal of the parent
whose sex is the same as the dreamer's.'

Because of the weakness of the child in relation to his
parents, he has to repress these hostile and love impulses.
This is necessary, said Freud, not only for the adaptation of
the child to its family but for its future adaptation to society.
We shall see later that, to make effective this repression, there
need to be socially acceptable avenues through which these
impulses may find expression. The adult, in other words,
must be provided with channels along which he can discharge
the emotional energy of these conflicting impulses. Freud
argued that the repression of these impulses, leading to the
dissolution of the Oedipus complex, is hastened by the
development of a *castration complex*. He wrote: 'It is not at
all uncommon for a little boy, who is beginning to play with
his penis and has not yet learned that he must conceal such
activities, to be threatened by his parents or nurses that his
member or his offending hand will be cut off.' He pointed

out that parents often admit making this threat but, in any case, children may concoct a threat of this kind from its knowledge that auto-erotic satisfactions are forbidden. In other words, the castration complex, the fear of being deprived of his penis, may develop from childish fantasies. For little girls, the castration complex is bound up with the feeling of being handicapped by the absence of a penis. Little girls quickly discover the physical difference between themselves and boys and this gives rise, said Freud, to a sense of deprivation only to be compensated for in adult life, through the specific feminine functions of child-bearing, home-making and so on. There is a difference in the rôle of the castration complex for the two sexes. Whereas the castration complex, in the boy, prepares the way for the dissolution of the Oedipus complex, almost the reverse takes place for the girl. The castration complex, in her case, precedes the formation of the Oedipus complex. The reason appears to be that the girl, like the boy, finds her first love-object in the mother, because the latter attends to her physical needs and feeds her. But with the realisation that she differs from the boy she feels herself at a disadvantage and tends to blame her mother. She consequently develops antagonistic feelings towards her mother and finds in the Oedipus complex a refuge.

This imputation of sexual desires to small children, particularly of an incestuous nature, naturally aroused considerable indignation when first propounded. Serious criticisms came from anthropologists like Malinowski who were not disturbed by the imputation of sexual life to children but whose own studies of other forms of culture did not confirm some important aspects of Freud's theory. Malinowski's *Sex and Repression in Savage Society* attacks the notion of the Oedipus complex as a universal factor in human societies. It certainly did not appear to be an active factor in the family relations of the Trobriand Islanders among whom he worked. The Freudian view of the Oedipus complex became modified when Freud developed his concepts of the ego, super-ego and id. The Oedipus complex was thought to 'pass away' with the development of the super-ego which takes over the rôle of the parent and other authorities in the child's life, as internalised processes. Empirically, I think one can sometimes discern a preference for the parent of opposite sex which might seem an indirect confirmation of the notion of the Oedipus complex. But I think it would be hard to say how far the preference develops spontaneously in children and how far it is due to the attentions of the parents. If the father fusses over his little girl more than he does over his little boy and the mother over the little boy more than the little girl, it is not surprising that children respond in a way which is consistent with some aspects of the Oedipus complex. In other words, the preference may not, at first, be of the child for the parent of opposite sex, but of the parent for the child of opposite sex.[6]

We have traced the development of sexual instincts through the first period of development to the stage where the child seeks its love-objects in the outer world. From five to twelve years of age follows a latency period, characterised by the absence of crude sexual interests and the development of the ego in harmony with the environment when the ego becomes differentiated from the id as a restraining and controlling force, adapting the impulses of the id to the requirements of reality.

During the second period of sexual importance – from twelve to eighteen years – the infantile impulses are revived, and the new flood of sexual life takes a course laid down in

[6] Since writing the above I have read the series of lectures given by Freud in Clark University, U.S.A., in 1909 and find that this point was already made by him. Thus: 'The child takes both of its parents, and more particularly one of them, as the object of its erotic wishes. In so doing, it usually follows some indication from its parents, whose affection bears the clearest characteristics of a sexual activity, even though of one that is inhibited in its aims. As a rule a father prefers his daughter and a mother her son; the child reacts to this by wishing, if he is a son, to take his father's place, and, if she is a daughter, her mother's.' (S. Freud, in *Two Short Accounts of Psycho-Analysis*, Penguin 1962).

This, I think, makes the notion of the Oedipus complex more credible and acceptable in terms of our Western culture where this kind of preference of father for daughter and mother for son is common.

earlier development. Thus it is extremely difficult to deal with problems in this period without knowing the determining features of the first.

The normal development of the sexual instincts may be arrested for several reasons. One of the component impulses may develop in advance of the others, and, becoming unduly strong, prevent further development of a normal pattern of integration. Or disappointment at one stage may lead to a turning back. A disappointed lover may return to his infantile mother-attachment, or indulge in auto-erotic practices.

This halting of the sexual development at a particular stage was called by Freud *fixation*. Fixation between parent and child, he suggested, plays a determining part in the choice of future love-objects. Thus in the case where the fixation is strong there is a tendency for the adult to choose as husband (or wife) somebody similar to the parent, who is identified with him. Where there is a very strong fixation, the tendency may be quite the reverse; for the identification of the potential love-object with the parent may be so close as to evoke the fear and disgust associated with incest. In this case, the tendency may be to choose one's husband or wife among people as different as possible from the parent upon whom one's sexual interest has become fixated. Where, however, one has chosen someone who becomes unconsciously associated with the parent of the opposite sex, the fear of incest may lead to impotence in sex relationship. The fear of incest may also make it difficult for a person to have a sex relationship with any member of the opposite sex – for all women or men who have become identified with the parent of opposite sex – and he (or she) seeks for love-objects among members of his (or her) own sex. This may take the overt form of homosexuality or be sublimated in strong friendships with other members of one's own sex.

The following two examples, taken from Brill's *Psycho-Analysis Its Theory and Practical Application*, shows the effects of identification with the parent of the *same* sex.

A refined young woman of twenty-four suffered from

psycho-sexual frigidity, but was sexually aroused when she saw a lame man. This was due to her identification with her mother, who had had an illicit love-affair with a man when the daughter was three or four years old. He sustained a fracture of his leg, and the mother found it necessary to make several journeys to see him. She took the daughter, to avoid gossip, and, although no conscious impression was made on the child at the time, she formed an unconscious association between lameness and sex.

In the other case, a young married woman exhibited a strong prostitution complex. While living with her husband she formed many illicit associations with men. She was an only daughter, and saw little of her father, whose affairs took him away frequently. As far back as she could remember, she recalled witnessing illicit love-affairs between her mother and other men. She herself married a man similar in type to her father and following the same occupation. She identified herself completely with her mother.

Love-objects determined by identifications of this kind are called *anaclitic* – literally, *leaning up against* – because they usually show a dependence on the protectiveness of the father or the food-providing qualities of the mother.

There is also another main class of love-objects known as narcissistic, depending on the following identifications:

(1) Identification with one's present self.
(2) Identification with one's past self.
(3) Identification with a part of oneself.
(4) Identification with what one would like to be.

In the first case, the love-object is sought among those who resemble oneself in some respect, physically or mentally. Thus a tall man may have eyes for no one but tall women.

In the second case, the sex instinct has become fixated on an earlier stage of one's existence, perhaps when one was more attractive or life was more pleasant, and there develops a tendency to choose a love-object from those who remind one of that phase. Disparity of ages in marriage may be due to this tendency in one of the partners. The third stage represents the possessive love which some parents have for children, seeing them as part of themselves. The children then are surrounded by protectiveness while the wife or husband may be starved of affection. In the last case, the person may be impelled by feelings of unworthiness resulting from a severe super-ego to choose someone with the qualities in which he, or she, feels deficient. The object of love is idealised and regarded worshipfully.

This brief account of the Freudian theory of sexual development can do little more than stress the complexity of this process. One's first reaction to Freud's notions may be a combination of bewilderment and scepticism. Yet one should be wary of rejecting these notions outright. We are becoming much more aware today, with research into sexual problems, of the complexity of man's sexual life, the astonishing variety of its expressions. We no longer tend to condemn out of hand, departures from what is socially accepted as normal sex practice as wicked and immoral. We are beginning to see that these departures, whether in the form of homosexuality or exhibitionism, have a history and background and require understanding. Freud may have exaggerated the rôle he makes sex play in our lives, particularly the nature of the development process through which, he argues, the sexual instinct passes. The details of this process are certainly not definitely established and are disputed by many competent researchers in child psychology. But, nonetheless, the fact that such a developmental process takes place forms the basis from which all serious students of child psychology begin today.

There is another aspect of Freud's sexual theories which has drawn bitter hostility. And that is the suggestion that man's varied cultural life derives a psychological strength from the sexual instincts. Sexual life, according to Freud, may find satisfaction and expression in a myriad of activities the

relationship of which to sexual needs is far from clear.
Freud's views are based upon two undeniable facts. The first
is that the sexual needs, unlike any other, are capable of
being satisfied, at least partly, in imagination. Thus while we
cannot satisfy our hunger or thirst by imaginatively picturing
food and drink, we can gain a measure of sexual satisfaction
in fantasy. We cannot satisfy our hunger or thirst by substitutes, or imaginatively, and live. The sexual instincts, if
denied direct satisfaction, can, on the other hand, turn to
substitute satisfactions and to fantasy. This is the fact that
gives Freud's theory a strong *apriori* basis.

The second point is that sexual life has been, and still is,
subject to more drastic repressions than any other group of
impulses. In our society, young people are physically ready
for a mature sex life at thirteen and fourteen but they are
expected to defer full sexual satisfaction for another four or
five years and then only to seek it in socially approved
circumstances. This deferment is aided by the teaching that
sex is a taboo subject, only to be discussed circumspectly. The
idea that there is something sinful and indecent in sex still
lingers in our times. Consider the taboo on words referring to
sex life. There is no parallel in respect of any other human
activity except those to do with excretion. And it is probable
that taboos connected with excretory functions derive from
their close physiological association with sexual functions.
Few of us can bring ourselves easily to use the four letter
words denoting these functions. Incidentally, it is interesting
to note in oneself introspective confirmation of a repressive
process, a resistance to the utterance of certain words; this
makes sense only in terms of Freudian theory.

If we take these two facts together, that sex desires can be
partly satisfied imaginatively and by substitute activities; and
that sex suffers, more than any other need, from repression,[7]
we can see the force of the Freudian argument that cultural
life draws a strength from repressed sexual energy. I do not

[7] The question why sex should be subject to this kind of repression will
be discussed later.

think that this is all that is involved in cultural activity –
alternative routes for sexual expression – nor do I think that
Freud thought this. But Freud's suggestion that through
these activities, repressed sexual impulses may find satisfaction, certainly throws an interesting light on many aspects
of literature and art. This is a point we shall take up later.
Here I would say that there is nothing derogatory in the
notion that culture – love of art, music, literature – has a
strong sexual root. It seems to me that much of the opposition
to this notion springs from the conviction that there is something insulting to human dignity in this view. If it turns out
to be true it only indicates how vastly more complex human
sex-life is than ordinarily believed to be. We already know
from the researches of Beach and others how different human
sex-life is from that of other animals in the larger part played
in it by the cerebral hemispheres. Whereas sex for most other
animals depends very largely on local stimulation by hor-
mone bodies of the sexual organs, in man this stimulation can
be largely absent without destroying man's capacity for
sexual desire. That the infinitely more complex nature of
man's sexual life may find a variety of expression in forms not
directly related to the physiological acts of sex, should neither
surprise nor depress us.

I shall conclude this chapter by considering a highly
speculative distinction made between the instincts, a distinction which, in the contemporary world, holds enormous
interest.

Freud at first divided instincts into two main groups; those
serving the preservation of the species, the sexual instincts as
described above, and those serving the preservation of the
individual, the ego instincts. These groups seemed to serve
purposes independent of each other, and could not be reduced to a common source. In conflict, the ego instincts acted
as the repressive forces and the sexual instincts as the repressed material.

This grouping was supplanted by another; the life instincts (sometimes called Eros), and the destructive (or death) instincts. Freud was led to construct the hypothesis of the two groups by consideration of the phenomena of sadism and masochism. By sadism is meant the obtaining of sexual satisfaction through the infliction of pain on the sexual object, while masochism involves the suffering of pain to gain sexual satisfaction. These two tendencies seemed explainable best on the hypothesis of a fusion between two kinds of instincts, the sexual and the destructive. All instinctive impulses, Freud believed, are made up of fusions of these instincts in various degrees.

Masochism, if we abstract its sexual component, argues the existence of a tendency towards self-destruction. Since the whole of the instincts originally were included within the personality, developing interest in outer objects later, masochism, the impulse to self-destruction, must be older, more fundamental, than sadism. In the latter case, the destructive impulses are no longer directed inwards towards the self, but outwards. They are converted into aggression. If the aggression is thwarted in the outer world, i.e. cannot find objects upon which to expend itself, it turns inwards once more threatening self-destruction. To avoid this it becomes essential to find objects in the outer world upon which to direct this aggression. 'We have to destroy other things and people,' wrote Freud,[8] 'in order not to destroy ourselves, in order to protect ourselves from the tendencies to self-destruction.'

In his letters to Einstein,[9] Freud advanced the view that war is the 'diversion of the destructive impulse towards the external world', and finds in it a 'biological justification'. 'We can but own,' he wrote, 'that they (the tendencies towards war) are really more akin to nature than our stand against them which in fact remains to be accounted for.' Another prominent psycho-analyst, Dr. Glover, wrote on the relation of war to pacifism. He contended that a 'large part of the

---

[3] *New Introductory Lectures*, p. 137.
[9] *Why War?* by Albert Einstein and S. Freud (Allen & Unwin, 1933).

energy that drives a peace organisation has precisely the same source of energy that lets loose war', and consequently pacifist measures tend to be uncertain because 'under conditions of stress' they reveal themselves as aggressive impulses.[10]

This Freudian view has aroused feelings of repugnance even among people sympathetic towards his theories in general. It seems to be saying that destructiveness is a natural component of man's psychology and if it is not turned out-wards it will lead to self-destruction. If this is true it certainly is consistent with much of man's history, replete with re-ligious and political persecutions, tortures and cruelties and the present hovering menace of nuclear destruction. But it would be a mistake to think that Freudian theory leads in-evitably to a pessimistic view of man's ability to cope with his aggressive impulses. Man's rational self, the product of inter-action between the strivings of the id for unconditional grati-fication and the exigencies of the outer world, holds the hope that he will be able to master those inner destructive forces and turn them to socially valuable ends. Freud himself had to rebuke those psycho-analysts who took too despairing a view of the possibilities of rational control and pointed out that, however weak the ego was in relation to the 'daemonic forces within us', the growth of knowledge and understand-ing about human psychology provided the best means of free-ing the ego from its enslavement to the purposes of the id. 'Where id was, there shall ego be,' he wrote. We may there-fore look upon Freud's dark picture of the forces of destruc-tion within us urging the world to mutual destruction as a warning of what could be if our rational selves do not take command.

[10] *War, Sadism and Pacifism* (Allen & Unwin, 1933).

3

Dreams and Analysis

Freud has brought dreams within the realms of scientific inquiry. Previously dreams had been the province of fortune-tellers, soothsayers and charlatans of every kind, and scientists had hardly considered it worth while to pay much attention to what seemed a happy hunting ground for those who preyed on the superstitious and ignorant. If they did give the matter a thought, they declared dream-life to be the product of a tired brain and left it at that.

Freud describes this attitude in a passage telling how dreams became part of psycho-analytic technique. 'One day the discovery was made that the symptoms of disease in certain nervous patients have meaning. It was upon this discovery that the psycho-analytic method of treatment was based. In this treatment it happened that patients, in speaking of their symptoms, also mentioned their dreams, whereupon the suspicion arose that these dreams too had meaning ... So dreams became the object of psycho-analytic research – another of these ordinary underrated occurrences, apparently of no practical value . . .'[1]

The general purpose of a dream, in psycho-analytic theory, is to ward off anything that might disturb sleep. A simple example is of the hungry man whose pangs of hunger, acting

[1] *Introductory Lectures*, p. 68 (Allen & Unwin).

as internal disturbing stimuli, threaten to waken him. He
thereupon dreams of partaking of a banquet, and thus, in the
imagined satisfaction of his hunger, preserves his sleep.
Familiar examples of external conditions being used in
dreams are the leaking hotwater bottles which give rise to
dreams about the sea and the buzzing of the alarm clock that
assumes, in a dream, the more soothing tinkle of bells. Thus
sleep is preserved while the disturbing stimuli have been incorporated in a dream.

In addition to its protective role, the dream, according to
Freud, embodies a wish-fulfilment denied in reality. An important part of analytic technique consists in the unravelling
of the dream as recounted by the dreamer, to find the wish
incorporated in it.

In this process, a distinction is made between the manifest
and the latent content of the dream. The latent content is the
real motive of the dream – the repressed mental processes
which lead up to it. In order to gain expression in consciousness, these unconscious processes use other ideas, images and
symbols as means of evading the repressing forces, the effec-
tiveness of which is somewhat relaxed in sleep. 'A dream is
the disguised fulfilment of a repressed wish,' wrote Freud, 'it
is a compromise between the demands of a repressed impulse
and the resistance of a censoring force in the ego.'

The actual presentations in the dream are known as the
manifest content, underlying which is the latent content with
the real significance of the dream. The task of the psycho-
analyst is to seek behind the dream as told by the dreamer
for the underlying unconscious processes responsible for
it.

Freud compared the dream-censorship which compels the
distortion of the latent content into the manifest content, to
the Press-Censorship which operates during a war. 'Take up
any political paper and you will find that here and there in
the text something is omitted, and in its place the blank
white of the paper meets your eye: ... On other occasions ...
the writer foreseeing which passages were likely to be ob-

jected to by the censor, has forestalled him by softening them
down ... contenting himself with hints and allusions to what
he really wants to write. In this case ... from the roundabout
and obscure mode of expression you can detect the fact that
... the author had the censorship in mind.'[2]

The mental process by which repressed material gains
access to consciousness is known as the *dream-work*. By its
means disturbing stimuli are worked into the dream and provide imagery in which the repressed material gains expression.

Let us now consider some of the means adopted by the
dream-work in transforming the latent into the manifest content of the dream.

By *condensation* said Freud, 'we mean to convey the fact
that the content of the manifest dream is less rich than that of
the latent thoughts – is, as it were, a kind of abbreviated
translation of the latter'.

It is a process whereby a number of elements in the latent
content which have some common characteristics are fused
together and represented in the manifest dream by one image
or idea. A person, in a dream, may be constituted of a fusion
of characteristics of several persons. We may dream, for
example, of someone who looks like Mr. Brown, walks like
Mr. Green, and dresses like Mr. White. Or a place called
Southpool, in our dream, may be a symbolic blending of two
experiences – one at Southend, and the other at Blackpool.
There is some associative bond between these people or
places in the latent content which allows of their blending in
the manifest content.

The process is very complex, for not only may several repressed impulses be represented by one element in the manifest dream, but one repressed impulse may express itself
through several manifest elements. There is what Freud described as an 'interlacing' between the manifest and latent
content, so that the meaning of each element in the manifest
dream often has to await the interpretation of the whole
dream.

---

[2] *Introductory Lectures*, p. 116.

Possibly the most important process of dreamwork is *displacement*. It is mainly responsible for the unintelligible nature of the manifest dream.

The emotional interest attaching to an important element in the latent content may be displaced on to another less important one so that the accent in the manifest dream is placed on unimportant elements. What, therefore, seems to be the central theme of the dream is really an insignificant factor, while the real meaning of the dream is vested in an inconspicuous element of the manifest dream. In a dream depicting a house, the ornate appearance of the doors and windows may draw attention from the really important element of the dream, namely a tiny chimney pot. 'Displacement,' said Freud, 'is the chief method employed in the process of dream-distortion, which the dream thoughts have to undergo under the influence of the censorship.'

By means of *dramatisation* the thoughts, in a dream, are given visual form, abstract ideas being represented by concrete objects. This is closely connected with displacement, for one of the causes for the choice of an idea upon which to displace the emotional tone of an important element will be the extent to which it permits the visual representation of the important element. 'The dream activity,' said Freud, 'does not hesitate promptly to recast the inflexible thought into another verbal form, even if it is a more unusual one, so long as this form makes dramatisation possible, and thus puts an end to the psychological distress caused by cramped thinking.'

The dream is presented as action, dramatically; considerations of space and time being ignored in the play of manifest ideas.

Finally, the process of *secondary elaboration* takes place at the moment of emerging from sleep and continues after. The dream is elaborated by the wakened censor, given coherence and a more logical form. Certain elements are more thoroughly disguised so that they will not disturb consciousness. The various elements in the manifest dream are related to one another so that the dream forms a whole, whereas, 'in general, we must refrain from attempting to explain one part of the manifest dream by another part, as though the dream were a coherent whole and a pragmatic representation'.

The effect of secondary elaboration is consequently to give an almost completely new form to the dream and further increase the difficulties of interpretation.

Repressed mental processes gain expression in dream life by the use of symbols. One object comes to stand for another because of some property the two have in common, though the association between them may be so slight that the conscious mind would not notice it. Essentially, symbolisation is the transference of emotional interest from one object to another. It is a process general to mankind, discernible in myths and religious ceremonies. The use of bread and wine to symbolise the body and blood of Jesus; the representation of justice by a blindfolded female with scales, are familiar to everyone.

In one respect, symbolisation of this kind may be considered as a response to the need for more or less primitive mentalities, to have ideas expressed in concrete form, but, when regarded as expressing unconscious processes, the symbols are rather disguises, for the most remotely associated objects are selected to represent repressed urges.

Certain symbols used in dreams occur so often as to have become recognised in Freudian theory as universal. Thus the human form is often symbolised as a house. If the walls are smooth, it is of a man. If there are ledges and balconies, a woman. Parents appear as kings and queens whereas brothers and sisters are symbolised as small animals, sometimes as vermin. Any reference to water, in a dream, symbolises birth and the relation between mother and child is symbolised by the act of falling into water or climbing out of it, or saving or being saved. Setting out on a journey symbolises dying. The sexual organs are symbolised by objects that resemble them in some aspect; the male organ by objects that have the property of penetrating – knives, daggers and so on – and such objects as sticks, umbrellas, trees, poles etc. The female genitalia are symbolised by objects which enclose a space – pits, hollows, jars, bottles, chests, and so on. The property of the male organ of erection is symbolised by activities that seem to defy gravitation, i.e. by flying in aeroplanes, balloons and so on. Or the dreamer himself may fly and if the dreamer is a woman, the flying may symbolise a repressed wish to be a man.[3]

The technique used in the process of psycho-analysis seems remarkably simple, but it demands skill and patience from the analyst, which only years of training can bring. It is known as free-association and consists of the following: The patient recounts a dream, or an experience, or an idea, or a pet theory, and the analyst asks the patient to let his mind play freely round it. He must make no effort to guide his thoughts, saying what associations appear in his consciousness. As one association recalls another, so the patient brings to light forgotten experiences. In the quiet of the analyst's room, the patient relaxes, and gives an account of himself and his dreams in his own manner. The analyst takes great care to avoid making suggestions by word or act, to the patient.

The analyst notes, as significant, pauses in the patient's account that seem to indicate repressed material. Much resistance is met with, as if the patient fears the revelation of his unconscious impulses, and it takes often many months to complete the analysis – months of patient and understanding handling.

An emotional relationship develops between the analyst and the patient, known as *transference*, involving the transferring to the analyst of emotions and impulses of unsatisfied earlier relationships. The patient thus relives the emotional situations underlying his difficulties and the analyst comes to represent now one, now the other, of the people towards

[3] The reader is referred to Freud's *Introductory Lectures*, for a fuller account of these symbols, see pp. 128-31.

whom the patient has had an emotional relationship. He may represent, for example, the patient's father, and the infantile attitude is directed towards him, with its contradictory emotions of love and hate. This double, or ambivalent attitude, in which an object or person is both loved and hated as a result of conflicting impulses, makes the task of the analyst a very delicate one. As Freud said: 'It is undeniable that in his endeavour to emerge victorious over the transference phenomenon the psycho-analyst is faced with the greatest difficulties, but it should not be forgotten that it is just these difficulties that render us the invaluable service of making the patient's buried and forgotten love-excitations current and manifest, for in the last resort one can be vanquished *in absentia or in effigie.*'

The final aim of the analyst is to make conscious the relationship of the transference, so that the patient recognises the rôle of the analyst and the nature of the conflicting emotions felt towards him. In so doing he is enabled to rid himself of dependence on the analyst and to recognise the root causes of his difficulties.

In estimating the use to which psycho-analytic technique can be put, Freud was extremely cautious. He frankly admits that the number of cures achieved in those cases treated analytically gives no ground for boasting. Indeed, he said, 'I do not think our successes can compete with those of Lourdes. There are so many more people who believe in the miracles of the Blessed Virgin than in the existence of the unconscious.'[4]

Discounting the ironic tone of this statement, there seems to be an underlying recognition of the rôle of suggestion in achieving cures, so that it would be difficult to say how far the success of Freud's technique was really due to its intrinsic value as a method rather than the confidence reposed in the analyst by the patient. But the importance of Freudian theory lies less in its therapeutic claims than in its value in giving us a deeper understanding of human nature. The

[4] *New Introductory Lectures,* p. 125.

importance of science, as we shall argue later, is not only that it gives us control and predictive power, it is that it gives us understanding, that it *explains* as well as points to possible forms of control. Freud's theory of dream activity, e.g., makes sense of dreams, explains them as a form of mental activity occurring when consciousness is minimal. One can see, in the light of his theory, how the fancies that pass through our minds when day-dreaming link up with night-dreams. We know how in day-dreaming we tend to realise hopes and wishes near the surface of consciousness; we see ourselves achieving fame and success or we re-order events so that we are reflected favourably in them. That this happens when we sleep and dream is, through Freudian theory, a meaningful proposition. Dr. J. A. C. Brown makes the point that much of Freudian theory makes sense because 'it appeared to be saying things that one had vaguely known all along'.[5] He quotes Professor Notcutt's argument in his *Psychology of Personality* that 'even those who regard dream symbolism as far-fetched or ridiculous know perectly well what symbolism means. A man dreamt that he came into the kitchen and, on opening the electric oven, saw that there was a bun inside on the tray; on waking up the dream seemed to him to be completely meaningless; yet, when at the local bar a soldier said to him, "My wife has a bun in the oven," he had no difficulty in knowing what he meant.'

There have been indirect confirmations of Freudian dream symbolism in research studies on sleep. One such study inquired into the way dream content was modified by meaningful verbal stimuli. Thus one subject was awakened after having had the name of his girl friend 'Jenny' played to him on a magnetic tape, over and over again, while he was sleeping. He was awakened and recalled a dream in which he opened a safe with a jemmy. The Freudian symbolism of this dream needs no interpretation. What is striking is the way in which an emotionally-loaded verbal stimulus gives rise to a dream-content which, while taking its departure from this

[5] *Freud and the Post-Freudians*, J. A. C. Brown (Penguin) 1962, p. 189.

verbal stimulus, manages to express latent emotional tendencies.[6]

Nevertheless, it may justly be argued that, while Freud established that dream-life could no longer be ignored as a field of scientific study, that it has meaning and is not merely the product of undirected mental activity, he exaggerated its role of wish-fulfilment. Perhaps the most that one could say is that dream activity is one way in which repressed wishes may find expression. But this does not mean that dream activity is *only* the fulfilment of repressed wishes, that there are not other factors involved. It seems a matter of everyday experience that one's fears and anxieties also find expression in dreams and while many of them may spring from repressed wishes, in the sense that the latter may be socially forbidden and therefore give rise to anxiety, others may have relation to more objective causes.

I have a friend, e.g., who was continuously unemployed during the thirties for over three years and he tells me that he has never quite got rid of a fear of unemployment and while he can control this fear during waking life, it sometimes emerges during sleep.

The fact is that much of waking life is subject to what Freudians prefer to term 'suppression' as distinct from 'repression' i.e. a conscious turning away from unwelcome thoughts and as, in sleep, conscious control is weaker, so thoughts that are suppressed, as well as repressed tendencies, may find expression.

[6] Personal communication from Ralph J. Berger, summarising his study for a Ph.D. thesis on a study of external stimuli and sleep.

Recent research into dreams is also highly consistent with Freudian theory. Thus Professor Nathaniel Kleitman has shown not only that we all dream even if we believe that we sometimes have dreamless sleeps but that we need to dream. A co-worker of Kleitman's, William Dement experimentally deprived a number of subjects of the opportunity to dream by awaking them as soon as it was clear from the variations in the Electroencephalograph record that a dream had commenced. They developed a pressure to dream, as if a safety valve had been closed; they became tense and anxious and when they were given the opportunity to sleep without interruption the extent of their dreaming increased. Thus the dream not only protects sleep by incorporating within itself disturbing stimuli but serves to discharge the tensions of repressed material, as Freud had maintained.

Marxism, being concerned with objectively determined events, particularly of a social nature, has little place for dreams in its theoretical structure. Nevertheless, as I shall try to show, dreams have a particular interest for a theory of knowledge. They are a form of a social thought, i.e. they are not involved in communication and therefore do not make use of the linguistic devices by which we communicate with one another and which, because of their high degree of abstraction, have their own forms of distortion. In any case, no study of human beings can ignore the reality of dream-life. That we can often satisfy in dream-life what may be denied us in external reality has a social significance whose importance remains to be explored.

4

Normal and Abnormal Psychology

An objection raised against psycho-analysis is that it bases its theories on observation made of abnormal or pathological cases. The Freudian answer is that the abnormal is removed from the normal by degrees only, and the tendencies in the one are but an exaggerated form of the tendencies in the other. The exaggerated quality of mental tendencies that the pathological cases present, merely makes it easier to study them. A closer observation of everyday behaviour reveals the same tendencies working, in a less pronounced fashion, in every human being.

The real danger lies in therapeutic practice. The psycho-therapist has to guard against a tendency to apply the categories of the abnormal to normal people – to see everyone as neurotic or psychotic – just because the latter show, in a moderate form, many of the behaviour patterns of abnormality.

In this chapter I propose to discuss some of the forms of behaviour in which unconscious tendencies seek to gain expression; some of the defence mechanisms used by the ego. I begin with a consideration of abnormal behaviour as a preliminary to a discussion of normal behaviour.

The main forms of abnormal behaviour are the neuroses and psychoses.

In neuroses, in the Freudian view, a situation has arisen where conflicting impulses are setting up an intolerable state of tension. Repression is too weak to deal with these impulses and a state of anxiety threatens. To avoid this, the ego develops the neurotic symptoms which either reinforce repression or give part outlet to the unconscious impulses. These symptoms provide a means of escape for the ego from the unconscious impulses, whose conflict gives rise to acute anxiety. Thus, during war many soldiers become prey to conflicting emotions and impulses. They may feel impelled to remove themselves as far as possible from the danger area but, at the same time, are restrained by the feelings of guilt that such impulses bring. To flee means disgrace. To stay means danger and possibly death. Here we see two conflicting tendencies. The ego has to face, on the one hand, the emotional demands raised by a danger situation, and, on the other, the moral strictures of the super ego which holds up a code of behaviour that makes flight painful to contemplate. A chance wound provides a way out. The victim develops a blindness or paralysis which renders him incapable of further active service. He is thereby enabled to satisfy the impulse to withdraw from the danger area and yet to do so without evoking feelings of guilt. Some conscious suffering may accompany the neurotic symptoms as a means of placating the super-ego. The blindness or paralysis is psycho-genic, i.e. of mental origin, for under hypnosis the sight or use of the affected part may often be restored, to disappear following the termination of the hypnotic state. The whole process of adopting the symptom is unconscious and without deliberate deceit. Such means of escape from an emotional conflict by the adoption of a physical disability in which the unfortunate ego seeks refuge, are called, in psycho-analytic language, conversion neuroses. The mental conflict is converted, as it were, into physical symptoms. On a more everyday non-neurotic level, we can see this tendency at work in the development of minor ailments – coughs, colds, headaches – that enable one to avoid unwelcome appointments or unpleasant tasks. The headache that excuses one from making a speech may seem to have come on spontaneously but it serves the purpose of relieving one of an unwelcome task.[1]

Another form of escape is provided by the compulsion neuroses. In this class are the obsessionals who feel compelled to perform acts which, in themselves, seem meaningless but symbolise the repressed impulses. Such acts as arranging, counting, touching things, have a protective value because they serve to prevent the performance of other acts which might arouse undesirable emotional associations. They may be reactions which seek, symbolically, to undo some previous action that has strong emotional significance. The compulsive acts may be accompanied by thoughts which may often seem trivial and pointless but which may serve to mask other emotionally important ideas. Failure to perform the actions, and efforts to banish the obsessional ideas, occasion great mental discomfort.

Freud gives a striking example of obsessional neurosis in his *Introductory Lectures*.[2] An intelligent girl of nineteen

---

[1] Such symptoms are sometimes referred to as hysterical, as forms of hysteria, in which physical symptoms have psychological origins. These symptoms appeared to be more marked in the First World War than in the Second. On the other hand, in the Second World War, there appeared to be a much greater frequency of what is termed 'psycho-somatic' disturbances. J. L. Halliday (*Psychological Medicine*, W. W. Norton Co., New York), suggests that this may be partly due to a change in fashion in diagnosis, *i.e.*, some disorders are now classified as psycho-somatic that were previously classified as hysterical. The difference between the application of the terms seems to lie chiefly in whether the organs and areas affected are under the control of the autonomic nervous system or the cerebrospinal part of the nervous system. In the former case, they are classified as psycho-somatic and in the latter as hysteria. L. R. Wolberg gives a striking piece of experimental evidence to show how conflict can lead to a hysterical sympton. In hypnotically susceptible subjects he produced conditions of post-hypnotic conflict. For example, in one case he told a subject that when he awakened he would find a bar of chocolate by his side and that he would have a strong desire to eat it. He was told that, at the same time, he would feel it was wrong to eat it, that it did not belong to him and that he must not eat it. It was stressed that when he awakened, he would remember these suggestions and would react to them. The subject awoke and seemed to develop a hysterical form of blindness for the chocolate. He was able to see everything else but strenuously denied that there was any chocolate present. He avoided conflict between his desire and his moral code by just not perceiving the chocolate.

[2] pp. 224-7.

became very depressed without any apparent cause. Before going to bed she went through an elaborate, compulsive ritual that caused her parents much distress. She insisted on silence at night and to achieve this she stopped the large clock in her room and removed her wrist-watch from it. Then flower-pots and vases were placed carefully together on the writing-table so that they could not fall down and disturb her sleep. She then insisted that the door between her bedroom and her parents' should remain open. Then followed an elaborate ritual concerning the bed. The bolster at the head of the bed had to be arranged so that it did not touch the back of the wooden bedstead. The pillow was placed across the bolster in exactly a diagonal position. The eiderdown had to be shaken so that all the feathers sank to the footend and then they were pressed out so that they were re-distributed evenly once more. 'Every action,' wrote Freud, 'is accompanied by the anxiety that it has not all been done properly; it must be tested and repeated; her doubts fix first upon one, then another, of the precautions; and the result is that one or two hours elapse before the girl herself can sleep, or lets the intimidated parents sleep.'

Freud's analysis of the ritual showed how they served a dual purpose, on the one hand of giving symbolic expression to repressed sexual wishes and, on the other, of serving as defences against them.

Freud pointed out that the precautions that this young girl took before going to bed had their parallel in normal life. Most people have a moderate form of routine preparatory to going to bed. It is only when these precautions become excessive and strongly compulsive, that they rate as neurotic symptoms. In the same way, minor compulsive acts such as avoiding cracks where paving stones meet, touching railings, counting stairs, hand-washing, are frequent in everyday life. When they begin seriously to disturb the pattern of life, causing distress when not performed, they indicate the presence of a neurosis.

Neurotic symptoms, then, are purposive. They are mechan-

isms by which the ego may defend itself against the demands
of the id. The anxiety with which they are generally accompanied represents the constant danger from within. Freud
distinguished three forms of anxiety, namely, objective
anxiety in which there exists a threat from outside;
neurotic anxiety in which the danger comes from within,
from the demands of the id; and moral anxiety set up by the
super-ego, when thoughts or actions conflict with its often
severe standards.

The neurotic person is often beset with anxieties which,
although he may see they are groundless or exaggerated in
terms of an external situation, he cannot shake off. The
anxiety may be 'free-floating'; that is, it may seem to be
directed at no particular situation but gives rise to a general
unease and apprehension. It may be phobic, taking the
form of fears regarding specific situations, of high places,
open spaces, enclosed spaces and so forth. The sufferer
may recognise that his fears are disproportionate, that he
exaggerates the threat from the external situation, but be
unable to control them. These feared situations may
have an association with unconscious impulses which they
threaten to trigger off. The phobia promotes avoiding
behaviour as a defence measure against the arousal of these
impulses.

The neurotic person, despite his unhappy condition, does
not completely lose touch with reality. He may seek help to
remedy his condition; he wants to find a way out of his insecurity and unhappiness. He has not sought to escape from
his problems by a complete distortion of his relationship to
the external world, or a complete withdrawal from it. He is
aware of his disability, has some insight into it and a sense of
social responsibility. Here lies his main difference from the
psychotic individual. In psychosis, there is withdrawal from
reality, or a thorough distortion of certain aspects of it. The
psychotic rarely acknowledges his disability. The world is as
it seems to him, a world in which phantasy becomes real. 'In
psychosis,' writes Freud, 'the turning away from reality is

brought about in two ways; either because the repressed unconscious is too strong, so that it overwhelms the conscious which tries to cling on to reality, or because reality has become so unbearably painful that the threatened ego, in a despairing gesture of opposition, throws itself into the arms of the unconscious impulses.'[3]

Classification of psychoses is somewhat obscure.[4] The main forms are Schizophrenia (formerly known as dementia praecox); Paranoia and Manic-Depression.

Schizophrenia is characterised by an incongruity between emotional and intellectual life. The patient may show excessive emotion over some trifling matter and seem completely indifferent over some circumstance that normally would be expected to arouse considerable emotion. Thus he might fly into a rage because a leaf fluttered down at his feet and seem unmoved at the announcement of the death of a close relative. It is this disharmony between intellectual and emotional life that has led to the description of schizophrenia as 'split mind'.[5] The schizophrenic has retreated from the everyday world into a world of his own. It is a world that may be peopled with odd delusions, or bizarre notions. Psychiatry distinguishes four main types of schizophrenia; *simple, hebephrenic, catatonic* and *paranoid*. They overlap in many respects with certain features predominating. The simple type is characterised by a dullness of personality, a withdrawal from reality with fantasy thinking. The hebephrenic

---

[3] S. Freud, *New Introductory Lectures on Psycho-Analysis*, p. 27.

[4] A widely used classification distinguishes between organic and functional psychoses. Organic psychoses are those in which there is a physical basis. They may be due to deterioration of the cortex as in senility, brain damage, inadequacy of blood supply to the brain, poisoning, etc. In the functional psychoses there is no evident organic basis. To them belong, e.g. schizophrenia and manic depressive psychoses. They may be regarded as disorders of attitude rather than structure, but it cannot be assumed, because no organic factors have been found, that none exists. Again, organic psychoses will express themselves in attitudes, so that the line of distinction cannot always be sharply drawn.

[5] This is a misleading description, confusing schizophrenia with multiple personalities in which the individual seems to have an alternation of personalities, one of which may be gay and mischievous and another solemn and proper, as in the famous Sally Beauchamp case studied by Morton Prince.

type is more marked for its fantastic delusions, auditory hallucinations, a certain silliness with giggling bouts and the use of neologisms in speech. The catatonic type fluctuates between states of stupor and excitement. In the stuporous conditions there is extreme withdrawal from reality. The patient seems totally oblivious of his surroundings and his own bodily needs. He does not speak and has to be treated as a baby. When he swings to a pattern of catatonic excitement his behaviour becomes impulsive and over-active. He seems to emerge from his stupor into this jarring over-activity, not because of some change in his external situation but in response to his own bizarre mental processes, the hallucinations and delusions that characterised his extreme withdrawals. In the paranoid type there is extreme suspicion of other people, a misinterpretation of trivialities, a strong delusion of persecution together with fairly active hallucinations.[6]

This last type resembles the form of psychosis known as paranoia and, indeed, some psychiatrists think it should be classified with it. In paranoia, however, there is little or no disturbance of the thinking process. There is acute suspiciousness. The paranoid sufferer may believe that the whole world is involved in a plot against him. He believes he is being persecuted, and regards the most innocent act and word as menacing his welfare. Actually he is being persecuted, and in a sense he is justified in regarding the least act and word with deepest suspicion, but the persecution is within him, and the acts and words which he distrusts are his own which may be acting as vehicles for the repressed, unconscious impulses which he fears. In other words, he is striving to escape from inner impulses by thrusting them on to the outer world, by ascribing them to other people, as a means of disowning them. He then regards the outer world as menacing his wel-

---

[6] Delusions and hallucinations are sometimes confused. A delusion is a false idea as, e.g. a false belief that people are plotting against one; a hallucination is a perceptual experience for which there is no objective cause, e.g. the experience of hearing voices or seeing people when there are no people present or speech being uttered.

fare. This process, known as projection, will be discussed in more detail later.

The whole process is quite logical once the preliminary projection of the unwelcome impulses on to the external world has been accomplished. Paranoids very often elaborate a remarkably coherent system of argument by which they justify their suspicions. One such case that came to my notice had an involved method of establishing that most of the recent murderers had intended him for the victim. Every murder of recent years had an element in it which he had seized on and definitely related to himself. Either he had been in the neighbourhood at the time, or his initials coincided with those of the victims – he met every objection with a fresh flood of evidence, complicatedly woven into a most convincing argument.

The last psychotic condition we shall consider briefly is the manic-depressive state. Everyone knows what it is to have changes of mood, to become excited at times and then depressed. Generally one can get the better of these moods, throw them off, or, at least, not allow them to take complete control. In the psychotic condition these moods take complete possession. They often seem to come without warning. In some cases, a long period of depression is followed by a sudden change to excitement of an intense kind. In other cases, there is an intervention of a relatively calm period which moves into sudden exhilaration of spirit. The pattern seems to vary from patient to patient. In the depressed state, the patient is often inactive, overcome by a deep melancholia. He feels intensely unworthy, indulges in self-accusations, goes off his food and is relatively immobile. This may change to the manic phase in which the patient becomes wildly active, talks volubly, has extravagant flights of ideas, seems bursting with energy. The cause of the condition is little understood. The Freudian interpretation is that, in the depressed state, an over-severe super-ego takes over 'has the ego at its mercy and applies the most severe moral standards to it'.[7]

[7] *New Introductory Lectures*, p. 83.

After a time 'the critical voice of the super-ego is silent, the ego is reinstated'.[8] The ego, once more in control and with the super-ego quietened 'finds itself in an ecstatic state of exaltation, it triumphs, as though the super-ego had lost all its power or had become merged with the ego, and thus liberated, manic ego gives itself up in a really uninhibited fashion to the satisfaction of all its desires'.[9]

Neuroses and psychoses, then, are defence mechanisms by which the ego seeks to protect itself from the demands of the id and, in some cases, placate an over-severe super-ego. They manifest, in extreme forms, tendencies common to all of us. In everyday life we employ mechanisms by which we seek to defend ourselves against unconscious impulses the expression of which conflict with conscious standards. They promote forms of behaviour which, in a moderate form, parallel much that can be found in neurosis and psychosis. A knowledge of these mechanisms is of first importance for an understanding of human behaviour both on a personal and social level. I propose, therefore, to finish this chapter with a brief account of the most important of them.

First, *reaction formation*. This is the development of attitudes and interests in conscious life that are the antithesis of repressed impulses. Attention is diverted from these impulses and repression of them consequently strengthened. A common reaction-formation is prudery of the militant kind. By active condemnation of anything to do with sex-nude postcards, dancing, courting couples, modern art, novels – a compromise is reached in which the unconscious sexual impulses are given part outlet in the pre-occupation with sexual matters, while, at the same time they are more effectively repressed because of the antithetical nature of that pre-occupation. There are, for example, people who keep watch in parks to detect 'indecent' behaviour; who tour seaside resorts to note disapprovingly the postcards displayed outside shops.

---

[8] *New Introductory Lectures*, p. 83.
[9] Ibid. p. 84.

Another familiar example is of the housewife whose continual dusting, polishing and cleaning make her the terror of those around her. Such excessive cleanliness is a reaction-formation to a strong impulse, in which dirt has an important significance.

Projection is a means of escaping from unconscious impulses. They are ascribed to persons or situations in the outer world and their internal threat is thus treated as external. Attack or flight then becomes possible, as in the case of a real external threat. By means of projection we tend to recognise in others, and to condemn, those impulses which we refuse to acknowledge in ourselves. An acute observer may often assess the character of an individual's unconscious tendencies by noting the things he most strongly condemns. The man, e.g. who is strongly critical of the faults of others may have a strong guilt complex of his own; the dishonest man may be constantly on the watch for dishonesty in others; the mistrustful lover may be projecting his own unfaithful tendencies.

An important method of giving expression to the sexual impulses is sublimation. The impulses are given aim and interests that are no longer directly sexual. They are de-sexualised and express themselves in a socially acceptable manner. In Freudian theory, many of the products of art, of literature and culture generally, depend upon a transformation of the energy of sex impulses. The advantage of sublimation is that it involves a minimum of repression, since it is not so much a defence mechanism erected by the ego against the demands of the id as a method of co-operation between the ego and the id. In this respect it is the opposite of reaction-formation. The contrast between reaction-formation and sublimation is illustrated by Ernest Jones as follows: 'The primitive tendency to self-display may be sublimated into a taking pleasure in self-prominence, either physically or in oratory, or, more indirectly still, as in the many varieties of fame-seeking, or, on the other hand, it may lead to reaction of modesty, shame, and the like (i.e. reaction-formation, R.O.).

The primitive pleasure all children take in dirt may be sublimated into painting, sculpture work, or cooking, or it may lead to the reaction of cleanliness, tidiness, and similar traits.'[10]

When sublimation occurs it means that the ego is sufficiently strong to utilise instinctive impulses for social purposes. Instead of flinching in the face of a reality that threatens to restrict the satisfaction of id impulses, the ego seeks in outer reality for modes of expression that give adequate outlet to id impulses without conflicting with social standards. Sublimation may be considered, therefore, as the main subjective source of social progress. Whether it can be directly encouraged is debatable largely because sublimation takes place on an unconscious level. But I think one is justified in arguing that an educational system, enlightened by psycho-analytic knowledge, would aim at measures to strengthen the ego and thus indirectly influence its capacity for sublimation. Alongside this, of course, would go the provision of opportunities for social development, a more rational economic set-up, matters to which we shall return after a consideration of Marxist theory.

One of the most widespread and easily recognisable of all mechanisms is *rationalisation*. It enables the performance of acts which otherwise might occasion mental discomfort, by reconciling them with conscious standards. This is done through a process of finding reasons for the action. Having found a reason which seems to justify the act in the light of conscious standards, it can then be performed without qualms or guilt feelings. Thus an armament manufacturer might excuse to himself the fact that his profits result from the deaths of innocent people by 'proving' that human nature demands war and that war is necessary to progress, as it stimulates inventions. This rationalising tendency is a defence against the logic that might compel an alteration in our mode of behaviour.

When a point of view has been adopted to accommodate

[10] Ernest Jones, *Papers on Psycho-Analysis* (Benn) 1918.

the expression of unconscious impulses by reconciling it to
conscious standards, any logical opposition will be greatly
resented as threatening an adjustment made between the id
and the ego. It points to the fact that people very often decide
an issue first, whether on politics, religion or some other
matter, on emotional grounds and then seek for reasons to
justify their decision. Discussion between two people in such
circumstances often resolves itself into a conflict between two
sets of rationalisations adopted for emotional ends. Each is
not so much listening to the other as thinking of 'reasons' to
strengthen his own defence mechanism. The 'open-minded'
person, particularly if he is fond of calling attention to that
quality, generally is more prone to rationalise than his
opponent who makes no such claim. The fact that anyone
insists strongly on his open-mindedness or broadmindedness
is often an indication that he feels a need to justify a particularly strongly emotionalised set of convictions. With this in
mind, much fruitless discussion can be avoided, particularly
on religious and political issues where the point of view,
having derived from emotional sources, is not likely to be
vanquished by logical argument. The strong need that some
people feel for the convictions they hold, leads them to
tolerate all kinds of excesses against those with whom they
disagree. The kindest and most sympathetic nature may be
transformed into a bloodthirsty type if its mental stability is
threatened by the assertion of views which, for emotional
reasons, it cannot tolerate.

The above-mentioned mechanisms are operative in everyday life, and with little difficulty one can discern them at
work amongst one's acquaintances and, with much greater
difficulty, in oneself. But even more common are the slips of
mind that reveal themselves in speech and writing and which
Freud called the 'psychopathology of everyday life'. He
showed that everyday examples of forgetfulness are not
accidental, but are strictly determined by the interference of
unconscious processes in conscious life.

Thus he argued that when a person of usually good

memory forgets an appointment, it is because he really had an unconscious reluctance to keep it. The doctor who said to his wealthy patient: 'I hope you will *not* soon leave your bed,' was motivated by an unconscious wish to go on treating her. Freud quotes the case of Ernest Jones who neglected to post a letter for some weeks. When he did eventually post it, he forgot to address it and received it back from the Dead Letter Office. After addressing it and taking it to the post he then discovered he had forgotten to stamp it.

Neuroses and psychoses are forms of maladjustment to social reality. For they characterise people who, in one way or another, get along badly in their personal and social relationships, are so insecure and unhappy as to find life becoming intolerable. The extent of this maladjustment, in contemporary society, is impressive. Thus, at the end of 1954, according to the Underwood Committee's Report on Maladjusted Children, two-fifths of the 480,000 hospital beds available were occupied by mentally ill or mentally deficient patients. Whether there is a quantitative relationship between neurosis and psychosis is not clear, i.e. whether a psychosis is an extreme form of neurosis is debatable. Eysenck, e.g., argues that they belong to different dimensions of personality tendencies. There seem, however, to be constitutional factors involved in both which may be responsive to stresses in the personal and social situation. Our society is particularly replete with circumstances which might well touch off neurotic and psychotic tendencies in the constitutionally sensitive. The goals of personal success, of increased possessions as marks of status; the drive to do better than one's neighbours, the encouragement of which forms an integral part of our educational system; economic and social uncertainties and struggles; the ever-present danger of nuclear destruction – all contribute towards the stresses that endanger the mental balance of those constitutionally sensitive. The Freudian analysis shows us what internal conflicts are involved in the development of neurosis and psychosis. We shall see later that the Marxian analysis tells us something of the external social situation that may stimulate and intensify those conflicts.

This completes my survey of the main concepts of Freudian theory.

I have been concerned to outline Freud's theory very much as he saw it, ignoring the deviations from the main stream. Freud was one of those thinkers of genius whose ideas remain alive and powerful for decades after their originators' deaths, while those of their would-be revisionists die with them. Thus Jungian and Adlerian theories are rapidly becoming of historical interest only, with the deaths of their authors.[11]

This does not mean that there have been no developments of Freudian theory but these have been largely in the field of therapy, in the application of basic Freudian theory in the clinical situation. We have already noticed a growing social awareness among latter-day Freudians, an attempt to see Freudian theory in terms of cultural and social determinants of human behaviour. This book is a contribution to this attempt, seeking to bring together in a fruitful unity the two major efforts of our times to understand human nature.

In general psychological theory, the main challenge to psycho-analysis comes from the Behaviourist approach, particularly where it is influenced by Pavlovian theory. As Pavlovian theory has been accepted by many Marxists as a framework for psychological theory, I propose to conclude this section with some comments on it.

Pavlov and Freud have more in common than is generally allowed. Both were strict monists, believing that human behaviour has a neuro-physiological basis. But while Freud urged that psychology could not wait for a complete neuro-physiological account of human behaviour, Pavlov and his followers argued that there could be no positive science of human behaviour without such an account.

Attempts to bridge the gap between neuro-physiology and

[11] This is probably truer of Adler than Jung whose work on personality types is still relevant though in no way in basic conflict with Freudian theory.

behaviour, however, have failed. Even such a thoroughgoing behaviourist as Clark C. Hull has stated that 'the gap between the minute anatomical and physiological account of the nervous system as at present known and what would be required for the construction of a reasonably adequate theory of molar behaviour is impassable'. It has become increasingly clear that psychology, to make progress, must establish itself on its own ground, with its own concepts and laws.

Pavlov suggested a way in which learning, under certain conditions, might take place; conditions in which an animal, passively held in the artificial conditions of a laboratory, 'learns' to respond to stimuli to which it had previously been indifferent. The dog's mouth waters at the sound of a bell. This has become a signal for food, having been rung simultaneously several times with the presentation of food. American psychologists, in particular, have extended and improved the conditioning process, elaborating a form known as *instrumental* conditioning, in which the animal performs some action, such as pressing a lever, or turning its head, which is instrumental in gaining it some reward.

What happens in the animal's brain, the kind of connections set up in the cortex, are still highly speculative matters. Pavlov's own account of these happenings is largely rejected by modern neuro-physiologists. In any case, the most that can be claimed for a theory of conditioning is that it might tell us something about the mechanisms by which new forms of behaviour are acquired – how one particular kind of learning takes place. It cannot, that is to say, supply a theory of behaviour but only throw light on a part – an important part – of it, namely, how new responses are acquired under given conditions. But we still have to ask – and this is particularly important for human behaviour – why a certain pattern of responses is learned, what needs it serves. For to know *how* it is acquired is not nearly enough.

We know, for example, that children need love and security, the care of their parents, if they are to grow into happy people. We know that neglect, poverty, lack of love,

unhappy homes, can lead to disaster in adult life. If needs are
neglected, patterns of behaviour may be acquired by which
forms of satisfaction of these neglected needs may be sought
which are harmful both to the person and society. It might,
in principle, be possible to describe the acquisition of these
patterns in terms of conditioning. But what we really want to
study are the needs that have been denied; the distortions in
behaviour patterns that result from their denial pose serious
problems for psychology, the answers to which cannot be
found in terms of conditioned reflexes.

Again, what light can a theory of conditioned reflexes
throw upon the appeal of religion? Freud, we shall see, saw
that religion offered illusory satisfaction to deeply felt needs.
It acts as a consolation for the tribulations of this life. His
theory of God as the projected memory-image of the father to
whom the individual turns for the love and protection that
he received as a child makes sense of the religious tendency,
but what sense can we make of it in terms of conditioning?

We know that the form of religion and moral practice will
be conditioned by the social milieu in which the individual
grows and an adequate theory of learning would study the
ways in which social influences impinge upon the growing
child. But the major problem remains: the nature of the
needs that seek for the illusory satisfactions of religion.

Freud described certain internal processes which shape the
individual's behaviour and which defy interpretation in
terms of conditioning. Consider such processes as projection
and rationalisation, described in this chapter. They help us
to understand what is happening in cases of racial and colour
prejudice; they point to latent hates and fears projected upon
minorities and then rationalised.

Freud formed his own concepts before such terms as
'model', 'intervening variables', 'constructs' became part of
the language of psychology. His concepts of repression, ego,
super-ego, id, are among the constructs with which he
worked. They have explanatory power because they link together otherwise disparate aspects of human behaviour. They

enable us to make sense of a vast range of human activity.

Freud hoped that it would be possible one day to find a neurological basis for his theories, remaining ever a firm believer in scientific monism. Pavlov's researches, I think, have provided an important stimulus in this direction. But this will not deprive psychology of the need to formulate its theories in its own terms. A neuro-physiological theory will tell us something about the mechanics of the neutral processes involved in behaviour. But the character of man's needs, their forms of satisfaction and frustration, will require more than neurological study for their elucidation. Neuro-physiological theory can only be a handmaiden to psychological theory. It cannot supply a psychological theory itself.

PART TWO

Freud and Marx

5
Primitive Society

In their views of the nature of primitive society, Freud and Marx have much in common. Both[1] put forward highly speculative theories for which, in the nature of the case, very little evidential material can be expected. They are imaginative reconstructions of the situation of primitive man which led to the impositions of taboos and limitations on his sexual life.

Freud took over a speculation of Darwin as to the character of the first human groups and made it the basis for his theory of the primal horde. Darwin has conjectured that man 'originally lived in small communities, each with a single wife, or, if powerful, with several, whom he jealously defended against all other men'.[2] This Freud developed into the theory that the primal horde was ruled over by a powerful male, who kept all the females for himself and compelled the younger males, under threat of castration, to restrain their sexual desires. From this theory, Freud was able to explain the elaborate system of taboos against incest which exists in primitive society, and the origin of totemism. In an absorbing book, *Totem and Tabu*, Freud traces the relationship between the totem, as referring to an animal or plant venerated as an ancestor, and the code of restrictions which

[1] This aspect of Marxism was developed largely by Marx's co-worker Engels and published in *The Origin of the Family*.
[2] *The Origin of Man*, Vol. II, p. 603.

he considers reflects the self-imposed limitations on incestuous desires which primitive man observes in deference to
the memory of the primal father.

A totem has been defined by J. G. Frazer as 'a class of
material objects which a savage regards with superstitious
respect, believing that there exists between him and every
member of the class an intimate and altogether special relationship. The connexion between a person and his totem is
mutually beneficent; the totem protects the man and the man
shows his respect for the totem in various ways, by not killing
it if it be an animal, and not cutting or gathering it if it be a
plant. As distinguished from a fetish, a totem is never an
isolated individual but always a class of objects, generally a
species of animals or of plants, more rarely a class of artificial
objects'.[3] The members of a totem group take the name of
their totem and believe that they are descended from it.
Within a tribe there may be several totem groups, and a
system of intermarriage exists, which precludes members of a
totem marrying or having sexual relations with members of
the same totem. This is a basic law of totemism. Members of a
totem must marry outside their own totem group, violation of
which rule being punished by the whole tribe. Violation of
the prohibition to eat or kill the totem animal or plant is
likewise punished severely, though the punishment, in this
case, takes place automatically. Thus an individual who discovered that he had accidentally eaten of a totem animal
would sicken and die. Freud quotes the following instance of
the severity of treatment meted out to violators of the marriage prohibition: 'In the Ta-Ta-thi tribe, New South Wales,
in the rare cases which occur, the man is killed, but the
woman is only beaten or speared, or both, till she is nearly
dead; the reason given for not actually killing her being that
she was probably coerced. Even in casual amours the clan
prohibitions are regarded with the utmost abhorrence and
are punished by death.'[4]

[3] *Totemism and Exogamy* (Hogarth Press), 1910.
[4] *Totem and Tabu*, p. 7 (Kegan Paul), 1936.

Periodically, the prohibitions against killing and eating the totem are lifted in the ceremony known as the totem feast. Every member participates and eats a piece of the sacrificed animal, thereby establishing a community with each other and the totem. The totem animal is then mourned with great wailings, after which there follows a festival in which all the totem prohibitions are disregarded. Free rein is permitted to all the pent-up desires; the prototype of the 'holiday spirit' prevails, in which all kinds of excesses are tolerated. Freud thinks that this gives an insight into the nature of the holiday of today, for it seems to be a recognised feature that the restraints of normal life should be thrown off and excesses indulged in which would be severely frowned upon at other times.

There are thus three main characteristics which Freud attempts to explain by means of his theory of the primal horde. Firstly, the members of a totem regard themselves as descended from a common ancestor. Secondly sexual relations within the totem are severely forbidden. And, thirdly, periodical totem feasts permit the lifting of these restrictions and are accompanied by contradictory features of mourning and gaiety. His explanation takes the following form: 'Psycho-analysis has revealed to us that the totem animal is really a substitute for the father, and this really explains the contradiction that it is usually forbidden to kill the totem animal, that the killing of it results in a holiday, and that the animal is killed and yet mourned. The ambivalent emotional attitude which today still marks the father-complex in our children, and so continues into adult life, also extended to the father substitutes of the totem animal.'[5]

This explanation Freud seeks to link with the Darwinian hypothesis of the primal horde, by means of a speculation which, he admits, 'may seem fantastic' but which, he claims, 'has the advantage of establishing an unexpected unity among a series of hitherto separated phenomena'. In the early human family, the younger males who had been driven out

[5] *Totem and Tabu*, pp. 235-6.

by their jealous father, banded together, killed and ate the father. 'This violent primal father,' wrote Freud, 'had surely been the envied and feared model for each of the brothers. Now they accomplished their identification with him by devouring him, and each acquired a part of his strength. The totem feast, which is perhaps mankind's first celebration, would be the repetition and commemoration of this memorable, criminal act with which so many things began – social organisation, moral restrictions, religion.' But after they had slain their father, and removed the obstacle from their sexual gratifications, the ambivalence of their attitude towards him asserted itself. They had also loved and admired him, and these feelings came to the fore with the satisfaction of their hate in his death. 'This took place in the form of remorse, a sense of guilt was formed which coincided here with the remorse generally felt. The dead now became stronger than the living had been, even as we observe it today in the destinies of men. What the father's presence had formerly prevented they themselves now prohibited.... They undid their deed by declaring that the killing of the father substitute was not allowed, and renounced the fruits of their deed by denying themselves the liberated women.'[6]

But the erection of the incest barrier was not performed without difficulties; for each brother was the rival of the other. Freud surmised that, for a time, a state of incestuous relationships may have occurred in which the fullest advantage of the freedom from the primal father was taken. Here we come to a point of contact with the view expounded by Engels in *The Origin of the Family*. The group marriage is the term he uses to indicate that all the women of one totem belong sexually to the men of another, a system of designation which Engels quotes approvingly from *Ancient Society* by L. H. Morgan. Morgan spent the greater part of his life among the Iroquois Indians, and was adopted into one of their tribes, the Senecas. His main work, *Ancient Society*, traces the development of human society from savagery,

[6] *Totem and Tabu*, p. 238.

through barbarism to civilisation. As a result of his researches among the Indians, and his study of material from sources the world over, he proclaimed that the conception of exogamy which was held by many anthropologists was based upon misunderstanding. Exogamy described the form of marriage which took place when members of a tribe were compelled to seek for wives outside their own tribe, while marrying within the tribe was described as endogamy. It was assumed that there existed two sharply separated marriage relationships, the exogamous and the endogamous, whose practice distinguished one tribe from another. But Morgan showed that the antithesis of exogamous and endogamous tribes had no existence in fact, but that within savage society the tribes were divided into a number of groups of 'gentes'. The men of a gens (singular of gentes) chose their wives *within* the tribe but outside their own gens. Thus while the tribe as a whole was endogamous, the gentes were exogamous. These gentes seem to correspond with the totem groups which we have been discussing in their essential prohibition of inter-marriage within the gens.

In the earliest form of this marriage relationship, it was surmised by Morgan and Engels, the men of a group exercised conjugal rights over all the women of another group. That is to say, the individual member of the group was not restricted to one woman, but was entitled to have sexual relations with any woman in the appropriate group. This constituted 'group marriage'. The children of such marriage called all the men who were entitled to have sexual relations with their mother, 'father', and all the women of their mothers' group 'mother'. Similarly, they called one another brother and sister. But this arrangement, while placing few restrictions on sexual life, was not, according to Engels, the earliest form of sexual relationships. He said: 'All the forms of the group marriage known to us are accompanied by such peculiarly complicated circumstances that they of necessity point to a preceding form of sexual intercourse, and hence in the last instance to a period of unrestricted sexual intercourse corresponding to a transition from the animal to man.'[7]

He asks: 'What does the term "unrestricted sexual intercourse" mean? Simply that the restrictions in force now were not observed formerly.... Unrestricted in the sense that the barriers drawn later on by custom did not yet exist.'[8]

What are the restrictions which later obtain in group marriage? Clearly they are the incest barriers by which intermarriage within the group is forbidden. If Freud's theory of the origin of totemism and exogamy is correct – that they were due to the slaying of the primal father – we should expect a period to intervene between the slaying and the imposition of incest taboos, during which the triumphant sons would unrestrictedly indulge their sexual appetites. As Freud observes, these restrictions were not imposed without difficulty, so that we can correlate Engels's view of a period òf 'unrestricted sexual intercourse', with Freud's belief concerning the slaying of the primal father.

But even more remarkable in similarity are the views of Engels and Freud on the conditions necessary for the formation of large social groups, which was prevented by the rivalry of the males. Freud put it thus: 'Though the brothers had joined forces in order to overcome the father, each was the other's rival among women. Each one wanted to have them all to himself like the father, and in the fight of each against the other, the new organisation would have perished. ... Thus there was nothing left for the brothers, if they wanted to live together, but to erect the incest prohibition – perhaps after many difficult experiences – through which they all equally renounced the women whom they desired.'[9]

Engels, who could only hint speculatively where Freud could build on later and fuller anthropological research, nevertheless brilliantly anticipated the Freudian view of repression as a condition for stability in social life. He wrote:

[7] *The Origin of the Family*, p. 43 (Charles Kerr), 1902.
[8] ibid., pp. 43-4.
[9] *Totem and Tabu*, pp. 238-9.

'But the mutual tolerance of the grown males, freedom from jealousy, was the first condition for the formation of such large and permanent groups, within which alone the transformation from beast to man could be accomplished.' He goes on to indicate that the group marriage, which was the first form of exogamous marriage, was marked by an absence of jealousy, for it provided that sexual satisfaction could be obtained from any woman in an appropriate group. 'And, indeed, what do we find to be the most ancient and original form of the family, undeniably traceable by history, and even found to-day here and there? The group marriage, that form in which whole groups of men and whole groups of women mutually belong to one another, leaving small scope for jealousy.'[10]

Thus we can quite easily correlate the view of Engels and Freud. The period of 'unrestricted sexual intercourse' to which the former refers is paralleled by the period succeeding the slaying of the primal father, wherein unrestricted satisfaction of sexual impulses became possible. And as Engels notes that 'mutual tolerance of the young males' was necessary to stabilise society, so Freud remarks that the brothers, to live together, had to erect the incest barriers. And, finally, the group marriage is equivalent to the first totem grouping, wherein mutual antagonisms and jealousies are repressed and sexual desires satisfied outside the totem group or gens.

To return to the theory of the primal father: its main merit is that it does enable the synthesising of much contradictory material. Freud was well aware of its speculative character, and said of it: 'I am used to being misunderstood and therefore do not think it superfluous to state clearly that in giving these deductions I am by no means oblivious of the complex nature of the phenomena which give rise to them; the only claim made is that a new factor has been added to the already known or still unrecognised origins of religion, morality and society, which was furnished by psycho-analytic experience.'[11]

---

[10] *Origin of the Family*, p. 42.
[11] *Totem and Tabu*, p. 261.

One objection that Freud considers in his above-mentioned book seems to me to have been partly answered by his own subsequent discovery of those mental tendencies that he groups under the heading of the super-ego. He formulated the objection thus: 'We let the sense of guilt for a deed survive for thousands of years, remaining effective in generations which could not have known anything of this deed. We allow an emotional process such as might have arisen among generations of sons that had been ill-treated by their fathers, to continue to new generations which had escaped such treatment by the very removal of the father.'[12]

The difficulty with this view is that it seems to require the belief in the inheritance of acquired mental dispositions, the transmission of the consequences of emotional experiences from one generation to another. And this runs directly contrary to accepted genetic theory. However, after writing *Totem and Tabu* Freud developed his view regarding the relationship between the child and parent so that his conception of the super-ego puts the matter in a clearer light. The super-ego is based on identifications with the parent; the assumption within the mind of the stern, censorious father of childhood days. But the father's stern attitude to the child is dictated largely by his own super-ego, which was formed through identifications with *his* father. In this way, the super-ego acts as the vehicle of tradition so that, through a series of identifications, the sense of guilt for the slaying of the primal father would reappear generations after the deed. In Christian doctrine, for example, the sense of guilt for an act of rebellion against the father (God) plays a central role. This sin is atoned for by the sacrifice of the son, who thereby, through the expiation of the crime, becomes as a god, with his father. In the Eucharist, the Christian totem feast, the body of the son is consumed, and those partaking are identified with the father, through the son, sharing in their holiness. But the doctrine of original sin requires that the sense of guilt for the primal revolt against God be transmitted from generation to generation.

And this, we see, is accounted for psychologically in the Freudian concept of the super-ego.

We have seen that the Freudian view emphasises the basic role of sexual factors in social organisation. That Engels also recognised the sexual basis of society is clear from his commendatory remarks on Morgan, as follows: 'Morgan deserves great credit for rediscovering and re-establishing in its main outlines this (sexual) foundation of our written history, and of finding in the sexual organisations of the North American Indians the key that opens all the unfathomable riddles of most ancient Greek, Roman, and German history.'[13]

But, while accepting the sexual basis of history, Engels insisted that 'under this formation based on sexual ties, the productivity of labour is developed more and more,' so that economic relationships tend to become the dominant characteristics of social organisation. This does not controvert the basic role of sexual factors, for the instinctive energy involved in these factors is susceptible of displacement, sublimation and other indirect forms of expression, as we saw in chapter four. The transference of sexual interest to the labour process is illustrated by Freud in regard to language, which, beginning as a means of summoning the sexual mate, later developed as a rhythmic stimulus to work. He said (quoting a philologist who arrived independently of psycho-analysis at these conclusions) 'that the first sounds uttered were a means of communication, and of summoning the sexual partner, and that in the later development the elements of speech were used as an accompaniment to the different kinds of work carried on by primitive man. This work was performed by associated efforts, to the sound of rhythmically repeated utterances, the effect of which was to transfer a sexual interest to the work. Primitive man thus made his work agreeable, so to speak, by treating it as the equivalent of, and substitute for, sexual activities. The word uttered during the communal

[13] Preface—*The Origin of the Family.*

work has therefore two meanings, the one referring to the sexual act, the other to the labour which had come to be equivalent to it. In time the word was dissociated from its sexual significance and its application confined to the work.'[14] Thus the view of Engels may be correlated with that of Freud with the recognition that the labour process provides a channel for displaced sexual energy. Perhaps a consideration of the role of repression may make this clearer.

In the history of society, repression is of basic importance. It is a necessary means of stabilising society as both Engels and Freud recognised. 'We believe,' said Freud, 'that civilisation has been built up, *under the pressure of the struggle for existence*, by sacrifices in gratification of the primitive impulses.'[15] But the repression of an impulse gives rise to a need for some conscious form of activity through which it can express itself, without disturbing the social organisation. The more society was dominated by sexual ties, the less need was there for displaced, or indirect, expression of sexual impulses, for they were not so repugnant to conscious standards. But Engels correlated the development of the labour process with the passing of the dominance of sexual ties. Engels naturally referred to the conscious, overt forms of sexual life when he spoke of 'sexual ties' rather than the unconscious impulses behind it. These ties, the marriage customs etc., are conscious socialised forms, we have seen, in which repressed desires find gratification. The 'unrestricted sexual intercourse' which, in Engels' view, characterised the earliest forms of human society, gave place to a more limited form of expression in the institution of marriage and society, thus passing from a form of organisation dominated by sexual ties to one wherein the labour process dominates. In other words, man became a working animal with the repression of his individual sexual strivings, for work involves social co-operation which is impossible without such repression. And here we come to the important question of the origin of repression. We have seen

[14] *Introductory Lectures*, p. 141.
[15] ibid., p. 17.

that it became necessary as a means of stabilising men's relationships within society, but the important point in connection with it is that it arose through the pressure of external circumstances. Freud, speculating on the origin of repression, considered it possible that it arose through the pressure of the ice-age, which drove human beings into more restricted territory, and made necessary the repression of antagonisms within the horde, in order that a more effective struggle might be waged against rival hordes for territory. Thus the inter-group antagonisms were diverted, through sheer economic necessity, towards other groups.

Even more clearly does Freud express the view that repression is a response to social and economic needs when he wrote: 'At bottom society's motive (for restraining the instinctive life) is economic; since it has not means enough to support life for its members without work on their part, it must see to it that the number of these members is restricted and their energies directed away from sexual activities on to their work – the eternal primordial struggle for existence, therefore persisting to the present day.'[16]

It might be argued that the theories of Freud and Marx regarding man's primitive ancestry are far too speculative to carry much scientific weight. And indeed many anthropologists are highly critical of them. They belong perhaps to the type of theory suggested by Hobbes, Rousseau and Locke to account for the origin of human society, interesting speculations deriving their importance chiefly from their explanatory function. I think that if we regard them as attempts to fill in the blanks, not so much in our knowledge of primitive man, but of pre-human man, their explanatory value is enhanced. If evolutionary theory means anything, we must hold that man had a pre-human ancestry. Among man's distinctive qualities is the capacity to think ahead, to refrain from immediate instinctual gratification for some future gain. In man, even today, this is not always easy. How much more difficult must it have been for these pre-human

[16] *Introductory Lectures*, p. 262.

ancestors, endowed with impelling instincts demanding immediate gratification and with a much less effective restraining mechanism. We can only guess as to the process by which man built up an effective social organisation with which to limit and redirect his instinctive life. We can be sure that this was a necessary stage in the transition from animal to human life. The theories of Freud and Marx concerning this transition carry conviction, I think, because they present, on a large, historical scale, what we can observe going on in the child growing into a social being. He has to learn to restrain his impulses, to limit his demands to fit in with the pattern of social life, to forego many personal ends that threaten social goals. This is the great merit of the Freudo-Marxist picture. It gives an account of the trials and difficulties of early childhood, both of the human individual and the human race.

6

Religion and Moral Theory

The theme of this book is that Marxism and psycho-analysis make complementary approaches to the study of human nature. Psycho-analysis lays stress on the subjective factors, the needs and strivings which lead men to activity, while Marxism is concerned with the external social situation through which this activity finds expression. This chapter considers this complementariness in relation to religious and moral thought. For nowhere is it shown to better effect.

But first I wish to anticipate an objection. It is that no attempt to describe the psychological and social factors involved in religious thought can tell us whether the claims that religion makes concerning God, creation, after-life and so on, are true or false. In other words, to say how it happens that people hold certain things to be true, does not tell us whether these things are true. And this I readily concede. We are only concerned with religion as a social and psychological force. Whether there are special religious truths and special methods for establishing them, are questions outside our inquiry. But what does fall within our inquiry is the fact that people have religious beliefs and the relation of these beliefs to the general pattern of social life.

For many people to live and work together, particularly in circumstances where inequalities of privilege and wealth hold potential stresses, ways of regulating their relationships are required. These may be by compulsion, through the state exercise of power, and through education and persuasive techniques by which people are brought to accept as natural and unquestionable certain patterns of behaviour. Religion belongs largely to this latter form of securing social uniformity of behaviour. It does so by laying down certain codes of behaviour, certain notions as to what should or should not be done, and securing their observance by invoking a superhuman sanction. In other words, religions have their most important social effects by saying: 'You should behave in such and such a way because this is how God wishes you to behave. If you do, you will be rewarded hereafter. If you don't, dire punishment awaits you.' This seems to be the basic social role of religion, to secure the acceptance of patterns of behaviour in the name of a superhuman sanction.

Religion depends, for its social effects, on the existence of important psychological characteristics in man. In the first place, there is the disposition to raise questions about the meaning of human existence; questions about the nature and purpose of life. These questions are not necessarily asked in a precise form and probably rarely get beyond a vague unease about the human situation but this capacity to think and feel about these problems seems a distinctively human property. Religion gives one kind of answer. Other kinds are offered by science and philosophy.

But it is not enough to say that religion offers answers to questions of human destiny. The important questions are: why do many people feel the need for the particular kind of answers given by religion; answers in terms of a God, creation, heaven and hell? And how do these answers enable religion to play its social role in the regulation of social relations, of contributing towards the reduction of social tension. With the first question Freudian theory is particularly concerned. With the second, Marxism concerns itself.

Marx saw religion as originally a reflection of the superiority of natural forces in man's mind. Primitive man, faced

with the perils of nature, assumed that there were supernatural forces which were responsible for the hazards of his
life. He would strive to propitiate these forces with gifts and
prayers, personifying them as beings with power to influence
his life for good and ill.

As the terrors of nature receded before man's growing
knowledge and conquests, the character of religion changed.
The main threat to man's security came instead from social
forces; the helplessness that man had felt in the face of
natural forces was replaced by a helplessness before economic
and social forces equally beyond his control. This is how
Engels expressed it: 'All religion, however, is nothing but
the fantastic reflection in men's minds of those external forces
which control their daily life; a reflection in which the
terrestrial forces assume the form of supernatural forces...
But it is not long before, side by side with the forces of
Nature, social forces begin to be active; forces which present
themselves to man as equally extraneous and at first equally
inexplicable, dominating them with the same apparent necessity as the forces of Nature themselves. The fantastic per-
sonifications which at first only reflected the mysterious forces
of Nature, at this point acquire social attributes, become
representatives of the forces of history.... We have already
seen, more than once, that in existing bourgeois society men
are dominated by the economic conditions created by themselves, by the means of production which they themselves
have produced, as if by an extraneous force. The actual basis
of religious reflex action therefore continues to exist, and
with it the religious reflex itself.'[1]

This Marxist view, then, sees religion as objectively due to
the dominating character of external reality, at first, natural
and then progressively social in character, before which man
feels weak and helpless. But we still need an explanation for
the form this religious reflex takes; why, i.e., man reacts to
this helplessness by personifying external forces and then
attempts to enlist the aid of the gods or God by prayer and

---

[1] *Anti-Dühring*, pp. 353-4 (Martin Lawrence), 1934.

ritual. The Marxist view seems to over-stress the reflex character of religion, ignoring the contribution of man's own mental
activity. If there were no active principle in man; if he just
passively reflected the world in his mental life, there would
be no impulse within him to compensate for his weakness
before natural and social forces by creating religion. We need,
therefore, to supplement this picture of the external forces
which lead man to look to religion for help, with an account
of the subjective factors which shape the character of the picture. And it is this that Freudian theory endeavours to do.

Freud distinguished three factors common to all religions.
Firstly, religion involves an account of the origin of the universe which derives from the individual's own picture of his
own creation. Secondly, it acts as a consolation for the tribulations of this life with assurances of an eventual happier one.
Thirdly, it gives precepts to guide the lives of men so that
they may merit the reward of consolation and after-life. How,
asks Freud, does religion come to combine these three
characteristics? He traces the theories of the creation of the
universe to the individual's picture of his own creation,
thus: 'The doctrine is that the universe was created by a
being similar to man, but greater in every respect, in power,
wisdom and strength of passion, in fact by an idealised
superman.... It is interesting to note that this creator of the
universe is always a single god, even when many gods are
believed in. Equally interesting is the fact that the creator is
nearly always a male, although there is no lack of indication
of the existence of female deities, and many mythologies
make the creation of the world begin precisely with a male
god triumphing over a female goddess, who is degraded into a
monster.... The rest of our enquiry is made easy because this
God-creator is openly called Father. Psycho-analysis concludes
that he is really the father, clothed in the grandeur in which
he once appeared to the small child. The religious man's
picture of the creation of the universe is the same as his
picture of his own creation.'[2]

[2] *New Introductory Lectures*, pp. 207-8.

We may combine the Marxist and Freudian view of religion in the following way. The helplessness which, as the Marxist view stresses, is objectively responsible for religion gives rise to a need for protection and guidance in face of the difficulties of the external world. This helplessness, according to Freudian theory, revives the childish dependence on the father since in childhood the father gave the guidance and protection that the child needed. But, of course, the adult no longer sees his father in quite the same light as when he was a child. He has discovered that his father possesses the limitations and frailties common to mankind. To his earthly father, therefore, he cannot turn for protection. But he still retains, in his unconscious, the memory-images of the father of childhood, the omnipotent father who punished and rewarded him in accordance with the way in which his commands and precepts were observed by the child. To this memory, the individual turns for protection and comfort when reality threatens to overwhelm him. This memory of a powerful father is projected upon the outer world and looked to, for protection. It is referred to as 'almighty father'. The religious person thus manifests, in exaggerated terms, the attitudes which, as a child, he maintained to his own earthly father. The heavenly father is all-powerful, all-knowing and very stern, yet full of love. In religion we see, therefore, the important rôle of the super-ego which is identified with the external forces controlling man's life. The 'fantastic reflection in men's minds of those forces' (as Engels put it) leads men to project the super-ego and then to seek its protection.

The importance of this Freudo-Marxist approach to religion lies in its explanatory value. We can see how it happens that men seek for the comfort and protection of a superhuman being, particularly in times of insecurity and trouble. We can understand why it is that so much of religion is phrased in terms reminiscent of the child-parent relationship, why God is presented, sometimes as a loving and kindly father and at other times as an autocratic arbitrary being, quick to anger. For these are the qualities with which the

young child endows his father, the father who at one moment
is loving and indulgent and at another demands unquestioning obedience – 'Do this because I say so.'

Religion, Freud likened to a neurosis through which man
passes in the course of his evolution. It is 'an attempt to get
control over the sensory world, in which we are placed, by
means of the wish world. . . . But it cannot achieve its end. Its
doctrines carry with them the stamp of the times in which
they originated, the ignorant childhood days of the human
race. Its consolations deserve no trust. Experience teaches us
that the world is not a nursery.'[3]

In like eloquent vein, Marx expressed himself on the hopes
that religion raises in people's hearts. Religion, he said, 'is the
sigh of a heavy-laden creature, the heart of a heartless world,
just as it is the spirit of spiritless conditions. It is the opium of
the people. The abolition of religion as the illusory happiness
of the people is a prerequisite for the attainments of real
happiness of the people.'

I began by saying that an account of the psychological and
social features of religion will not tell us whether there are
such things as religious truths. Many people who may accept
much of the foregoing Freudian and Marxist analysis of the
psycho-social relevance of religion may yet object that it
ignores certain basic qualities of religion, in particular, that
religion satisfies certain spiritual demands of our nature
and leads us to truths about God and our relation to Him.
It may be true, it may be conceded, that we tend to project
upon God attitudes, fears, loves, that we felt towards the
father of our childhood days but this is not the whole story.
Our belief in the existence of God who is the source and support of our own existence, does not depend only upon these
projections. There is such a thing as religious experience in
which there is a revelation of truths that no Freudian-
Marxist analysis can dispel.

I can only reply that this may be so but, so far, no tech-

[3] *New Introductory Lectures*, p. 215.

nique – logical, philosophical, or scientific, has been devised
for discriminating illusion from reality in these matters. The
claim to possess the special kind of truth called religious truth
interests the psychologist perhaps more than the sociologist.
He will agree that he is in no position to pronounce upon the
validity of such claims. But it is a matter of psychological
interest that the religious man tends to respect only his own
certainties; the certainties of those who do not share his particular religious views are regarded as delusive, the product of
ignorance and confusion. I think the psychologist is entitled
to look into this matter of conflicting certainties. The
Freudian, for example, will tend to explain the uncompromising nature of the feeling of religious certainty as due
to the joint effect of super-ego and id demands. For it is of the
nature of the id to be uncompromising and absolute and of
the super-ego to vest power in some overriding authority.

The Freudian and Marxist views on religion thus closely
interlock. They both see it as belonging to childhood – the
childhood of the individual and the childhood of the race.

We turn now to consider Freudian and Marxist theory in
relation to moral theory and practice.

The Freudian view follows closely the view already out-
lined on religion; for Freud related the moral imperatives,
the promptings of conscience and the notions of right and
wrong to the activity of the super-ego. 'The prohibitions and
commands of his parents,' wrote Freud, 'live on in his breast
as his moral conscience.' What Freud has stressed is that
people are introduced to moral notions in terms of a system of
rewards and punishments. As children, they learn to associate
'good' with what the parents approve and 'bad' with what
they disapprove. The parents' guidance and authority, at first
exerted as external influences on the child's behaviour, become incorporated within the child's mind, constituting
therein a form of moral censorship. But the parents, themselves, reflect in their prohibitions, the pressures of society.
They transmit to the child the standards of their social group,
investing them with emotional significance, so that what is

socially considered impermissible connotes, for the child, the threat of loss of parental love.

In contrast, Marxism approaches the problem of morality in terms of these social standards. And in a society that is class-divided, it stresses the importance that class interest plays in determining these standards. This stress of Marxism on the role of class interests in moral thinking, has led to a serious misconception about Marxist moral theory. It is widely believed that Marxism dismisses all moral notions as 'relative' to the interests of this or that class; that what promotes the interest of a class is seen by its members as 'good' and what hinders its interests as 'bad', and this is all that 'good' and 'bad' can mean.

This view is often read into the writings both of Engels and Marx largely because their moral theory is implicit rather than explicit in these writings. In assessing the work of any thinker, one needs to get the feeling of what he is trying to say; to see passages in his works which may be obscure or ambiguous, in the light of his general aim. It is always possible to take a passage here and there and use it as a basis to interpret the whole of a thinker's outlook and produce thereby a distorted confabulation. If, on the other hand, one makes an effort to relate Marx's moral theory to his general theory about the nature of society, it becomes clear that there is no social relativism of the kind noted above, involved.

One must distinguish a general and specific sense in which moral theory is implied in Marxism.

In its general sense, moral theory in Marxism is related to its overall view of the nature of society, a view that has many points of resemblance with Aristotle's. For Aristotle, the *polis* was the natural way of living for man, because it provided the means by which human nature could develop its specifically human characteristics. A man who lives outside society, said Aristotle, is either a beast or a god. With this, at least in respect of the first part of the disjunction, Marx would have agreed.

If we pose the Aristotelian question – what is the function of society? – what is it for? – we can find in the answer that

Marx gave, the key to his general ethical theory. For Marx, society was man's way of winning his livelihood, of gaining his freedom from the domination of natural forces. It was for him, as for Aristotle, the means by which man may develop his humanity. In this consists the excellence of society, its good. The function of a thing in Aristotle's sense, is the expression of its distinctive characteristics, the performance of an activity which belongs peculiarly to it. Just as we can arrange objects in an order, so we can compare societies in respect of their function. Of two fountain pens we can say that one is better than another, if it writes more smoothly, holds more ink and so forth. And, in a sense, we can build a picture of the ideal fountain-pen by characterising the properties we look for in a fountain pen. In a similar way, we can speak of one society being better than another, of approaching nearer to the ideal society. We catch glimpses of the ideal society implied in Marxist theory as when Marx looked forward to the day when co-operation would have replaced class-struggle; when the 'narrow horizon of bourgeois right' has been crossed and 'society inscribes on its banner: From each according to his ability, to each according to his needs!'

Marx's picture of the good for man being realised in a classless society based upon a high level of production, is markedly different from the political ideal of Aristotle, an ideal described by Professor Taylor as 'of a small but leisured and highly cultivated aristocracy without large fortunes or any remarkable differences in material wealth, free from the spirit of adventure and enterprise, pursuing the arts and sciences quietly while its material needs are supplied by the labour of a class excluded from citizenship, kindly treated but without prospects'. But Marx, who had a high admiration for Aristotle, regarding him as the greatest of the ancient philosophers, would have been the first to acknowledge that Aristotle's idea needs to be seen in the context of the historical circumstances in which he lived and not in the light of present-day possibilities of life.

Marx was not so much concerned with saying what the

good for man is as with saying how it could be realised in
society. He was interested, in other words, in the concrete
realisation of the conditions in which men could achieve
their good, rather than in an abstract characterisation of this
good. He saw this good basically as the destruction of man's
enslavement to natural and economic forces, the ending of
conditions in which, in Kant's phrase, men treated one
another as means rather than ends. But he went further than
Kant. For he pointed out that the treatment of men as means
rather than as ends was associated with economic conditions
that forced some men to make use of others as means of enriching themselves, of securing power and privilege for themselves. Marx spoke of the 'categorical imperative to overthrow
all conditions in which man is a degraded, servile, neglected,
contemptible being'.

It is against this general view which sees man's good in the
destruction of natural and economic conditions that limit his
life, that the more specific Marxist view of the class nature of
morality must be considered. This more specific view of
morality was expressed by Engels as follows: 'We reject every
attempt to impose on us any moral dogma whatsoever as an
eternal, ultimate and forever immutable moral law ... we
maintain ... that all former moral theories are the product,
in the last analysis, of the economic stage which society has
reached at that particular epoch. And as society has hitherto
moved in class antagonisms morality was already a class
morality.' Here Engels called attention to the ideological
aspect of morality, the fact that morality can be used to protect and justify particular class interests. He argued that so
long as society is divided into ruling and ruled classes, the
application of moral rules tends to be narrowed into the
protection of class interests or to bear more heavily on some
sections of society than others. Within the present society, for
example it is considered wrong for a rich man as well as a
poor one to steal food but, owing to the more favourable
economic circumstances of the rich man, the moral rule 'do
not steal' has only formal application to him.

The notion of morality implies universality of application and moral philosophers generally formulate moral rules in universal terms. But such rules, Marxism argues, remain abstract and empty formulations, so long as the material conditions for their universal application are lacking.

Marxism, then, implies an ethical standpoint which sees the realisation of the good for men in their progressive liberation from the natural and social limitations on their human development. As moralist, Marx thunders against the exploitation of man by man. As scientist, he strives to set aside moral presuppositions in his analysis of society. But this moral standpoint breaks through again and again. As Schumpeter put it: 'the cold metal of economic theory is in Marx's pages immersed in such a wealth of steaming phrases as to acquire a temperature not naturally its own.' But he rightly warns against any tendency to shrug one's shoulders at Marx's claim to be considered an analyst in the scientific sense, because of these phrases. They do not, he points out, affect the nature of the analysis.

The failure to recognise the ethical implications of Marxism is responsible for some of the most serious mis-representations of the Marxist viewpoint. An example of this is contained in Professor K. R. Popper's criticism of Marxism in volume two of *The Open Society and Its Enemies*, in which he ascribes ethical relativism to Marxism. The ethical principle on which Marxism proceeds, he says, is summed up in the slogan: 'Adopt the moral system of the future!' Popper pictures Marx as saying to himself: 'I am able to see that the bourgeoisie is bound to disappear, and that the proletariat, and with it a new system of morals, is about to win. I see this development is inevitable. It would be madness to resist it, just as it would be madness to attempt to resist the law of gravity. This is why my fundamental decision is in favour of the proletariat and of its morality. And this decision is based on scientific foresight, on scientific historical prophecy.'[4]

[4] pp. 191/2.

In other words Marx desired socialism only because he thought it belonged to the ascertainable future. It is conceivable that the ascertainable future might have appeared as a much less desirable state of affairs, nevertheless – says Popper – he would have felt bound to say: 'adopt the moral code which will speed its realisation'. Thus Marxism, according to Popper, involves a moral futurism, the view that 'coming might is right.'

The short answer to Popper is that Marx was led to an examination of the capitalist society of his day just because it imposed serious limitations upon the lives of the greater part of society. That he thought such a study should be a scientific one has misled Popper into thinking that it was only as a scientist that Marx approached his task and not as a human being strongly moved by the evils of the capitalist society of his time. There is here a misconception by Popper of the rôle of science in the discovery of laws. A scientist does not seek for laws in order to warn mankind that it would be madness to resist them. The purpose of scientific discovery is not to underline man's helplessness but to help him forward in his efforts to subordinate nature to his ends. The 'inexorable' law of gravitation does not root man to earth's surface. He makes his aeroplanes with due regard for the law. He learns what events are covered by the law, how they are interrelated and is thereby in a position to work out means of circumventing, of neutralising, of utilising, of co-operating with, the law. Marx's compassion for the underdog caused him to seek to remedy the evils of their lives in a juster social system. His training as a scientist taught him to look for the laws of social change so that the reconstruction of society along more humane lines might have a rational basis.

We can now see how well the Marxist and Freudian views of ethics complement one another. The Freudian view, we have seen, ascribes the imperatives of morality, the sense that certain actions ought to be done and are right, to the compulsions of the super-ego. But this is not the whole story. For, as Freud pointed out, psychological development involves the replacement of the super-ego morality by the morality of the ego. In other words, the mature person who has outgrown the emotional demands of childhood and whose judgments are determined by reality considerations, develops a morality consistent with these considerations. He ceases to be governed by egocentric demands and becomes socially orientated. He begins to think in universal terms, to think for others as well as for himself, to become socially conscious. This account of psychological development, from the egocentricity of childhood to the social consciousness of adulthood, constitutes the main Freudian contribution to moral theory. But, the Freudians are quick to point out, it is rare for this process to take place smoothly and completely. Contemporary life tends to distort, hamper and stunt this growth of rational qualities of life.

The contribution of Marxism is to stress the social relevance of morality, the fact that one society is morally better than another to the extent that it provides the milieu in which men can approach their full human stature. Together, Freudian and Marxist theory present a comprehensive picture of the emergence and growth of moral thinking in man.

7

Social Development

Marxism is an account of the factors that determine the development of society. But society is not some abstract entity existing over and above the people composing it. It is a name for the totality of relationships in which people live. It has been aptly defined by Ginsberg as 'the web or tissue of human interactions and interrelations'. These social relations express the way men do things together, the kind of antagonisms and conflicts which take place among them, the institutions and rules of conduct they set up to regulate their interactions. Hence, in studying the development of society we are studying changes in people's behaviour, in the things they think and do. Hence, Marxism, in studying the changing patterns of people's behaviour in response to changes in their living conditions must imply a psychological theory, a theory of the kind of relationship existing between people's mental processes and the external conditions of their lives. This is a point to which we shall return. Here we note only that precisely because it aims to tell us what patterns of thought and action result from particular changes in the social world in which man lives, Marxism necessarily makes certain psychological assumptions. But before considering these assumptions let us see what Marxism has to say about the external factors that shape and condition man's behaviour.

The Marxist theory of social change is known as the materialist conception of history or historical materialism. As a preliminary to a sketch of those aspects of this theory that are relevant for our discussion I propose to describe some of the central terms in which this theory is expressed.

The process by which men obtain their means of living from the external world, namely their food, clothing and shelter, is variously termed by Marx, the *productive process*, the *mode of production*, the *method of production*. It includes broadly two groups of factors: those concerning the role of men in their productive process, sometimes referred to as the *subjective factors*; and those concerning the inanimate factors, referred to as the *objective factors*. The subjective factors comprise the distinctively human activity by which man acts upon nature, called by Marx *labour*. 'Labour,' he wrote, 'is, in the first place, a process in which both man and Nature participate and in which man, of his own accord, starts, regulates and controls the material reactions between himself and Nature. He opposes himself to Nature as one of her own forces, setting in motion arms and legs, heads and hands, the natural forces of his body, in order to appropriate Nature's production in a form adapted to his own wants.'[1]

The distinctively human character of labour is stressed as follows: 'We presuppose labour in a form that stamps it as exclusively human. A spider conducts operations that resemble those of a weaver, and a bee puts to shame many an architect in a construction of her cells. But what distinguishes the worst architect from the best of bees is this, that the architect raises his structure in imagination before he erects it in reality.'[2]

Further, the subjective factors connote the relations in which men stand to one another in their productive activities, the nature of the division of labour among them, the manner in which the proceeds of production are divided among them, the property relations, the kind of organisations

[1] Karl Marx, *Capital*, Vol. I (translated by Moore & Aveling), p. 156-7.
[2] ibid., p. 157. Dent—1933.

such as trades unions, cartels, co-operative societies that
directly affect productive activities: in short, the sum of relationships directly involved in the productive life of society.

It is within these relationships, said Marx, that production
goes on. 'In production,' he wrote, 'men not only act on
Nature but also on one another. They produce by co-operating in a certain way and mutually exchanging their activities.
In order to produce, they enter into definite connections and
relations with one another and only within these social
connections and relations do their actions on nature, does
production, take place.'

The objective, non-human factors comprise (a) the naturally given objects of nature, viz., the soil, forests, fish, ore,
animals, etc., raw materials such as felled timber, mined coal,
cultivated seeds and (b) the instruments of labour. These
objective factors are sometimes referred to by Marx collec-
tively as the *means of production* and sometimes as the *forces
of production*.

I propose now to give an account of the historical process as
seen by Marx. As this aspect of Marxist theory is nowhere
worked out fully in the writings of Marx and Engels, such an
account must necessarily be interpretative, seeking to capture
the meaning which these writers had in mind, making
explicit matters which are implied rather than stated.

Marxist historical theory regards the important changes
that have taken place in history and which have led to new
social forms, as primarily the consequence of changes in the
productive process by which men get their living. Men, unlike other animals, do not remain passive in relation to their
geographical environment. To wrest their living from it, they
act co-operatively, learning from experience and discovery
new and more efficient ways of organising their efforts; they
learn to construct tools, to irrigate the soil, to clear forests, to
gain from Nature more than she voluntarily offers. Men's environment ceases to be solely conditioned by the natural
qualities of soil, climate, etc. An economic environment develops which, based upon the original, natural environment,

bears witness to men's co-operative efforts to raise themselves above the level of existence permitted by natural conditions.

Society, then, from the Marxist viewpoint, is the organisational means by which men co-operate in the tasks of winning their livelihoods. Man wages his struggle for existence by means of a productive process. This is central in Marxist theory. This productive process requires that men stand in such relationships to one another as make its operation most effective. In primitive societies the truth of this is unmistakeable. The structure of a hunting group is necessarily different from that of an agricultural group. The relations among its members, their tasks and duties, will differ. Customs and general rules of behaviour will reflect these differences. An interesting example of this was given by the Marxist writer, G. Plekhanov. The Masai, in eastern equatorial Africa, he wrote, had not passed beyond a pastoral stage in social life. Their means of living were very primitive, yielding barely enough to live on. Hence they had no use for prisoners-of-war. For these would simply have been an additional burden on their existing slender means. So they showed no mercy to their prisoners-of-war, killing all who fell into their hands. Their neighbours, the Wakamba, however, had reached an agricultural stage. They had use for additional labour, for it meant more workers in the fields and a bigger surplus. Hence they converted their prisoners-of-war into slaves. They were able, that is to say, to treat their prisoners more humanely because they had reached a higher level of production. There was an interesting relation, bearing out the Marxist theory, between their moral code and their level of production – a matter to which we shall return. A recent study[3] of the Bushmen of the Kalahari Desert describes the relationship between their social structure and the scarcity of food and water. They live in small family groups around water holes as large groups would speedily reduce their food supplies. The hunters among them play a dominant rôle because upon them devolves the responsibility for tracking and killing the

[3] Elizabeth Thomas, *The Harmless People* (Secker and Warburg), 1959.

sparse game and leading them to the water-holes. Their
sexual codes are extremely severe, promiscuity of any kind
being strictly forbidden, a direct requirement of the need to
keep their numbers small. Indeed, a nursing mother who
becomes pregnant is expected to kill the second child.

With the discovery of new methods of production, new
social relationships may come into being, relationships within
which the new methods of production may function more
smoothly. Professor Acton, in a study of the Materialist Conception of History, makes the suggestion that the relationship between the conditions of production and the methods,
or forces, of production is, in a sense, a logically necessary
one. He illustrates his point by imagining a society of fisher-
men using small canoes each paddled by one man. 'The productive forces are the men paddling their individual canoes,
and individuals fishing from them. The productive relationships are their putting out to sea individually and working as
independent individuals.'

He then supposes that someone builds a larger sailing
vessel, that is, brings into being new productive forces. This,
he says, 'will bring with it a change in the productive relationships, for the new craft will require someone to man the
sails, someone to steer, and perhaps several men to cast large
nets. Now in what way does the new invention bring with it
new productive relationships? It seems to me that, in talking
of the new invention, we are at the same time talking of new
job-relationships. In designing the large sailing vessel, the in-
ventor was also arranging for new functions to be performed. . . . When, therefore, it is said that any considerable
changes in productive forces must bring about changes in
productive relationships, the "must" indicates a tautology,
though perhaps an interesting one. For it does seem to improve our insight into the workings of society to see that producing goods is not merely a relationship of individual men
and machines to Nature, but also of men to one another.'[4]

[4] H. B. Acton, *The Materialist Conception of History* in *Proceedings of
the Aristotelian Society*, Vol. LII, 1951/2.

This illustration of Professor Acton raises an important issue in Marxist theory. For the Marxist argues that, while one may recognise that changes in productive forces require changes in productive relations, it often happens that the latter changes lag behind the former. There is, that is to say, no automatic adjustment of the conditions of production to changes in the method of production. And the Marxist explains this lag by reference to an important factor in the conditions of production not discussed by Professor Acton, namely the class structure of society arising from the property relations of society.

In a simple society such as envisaged by Professor Acton, this factor might not be so important. But in a complex society in which the existing social structure brings important privileges to some sections of society, the adjustment of the conditions of production to the new forces of production may be considerably hampered. This is the point of the Marxist insistence on the contradiction between the conditions of production and the growing forces of production. Marx argued, for example, that the development of the capitalist mode of production was hindered by feudal social relations, local privileges and privileges of birth. It required conditions of free competition, freedom of movement of labour, political rights of the growing capitalist class, in which to flourish. In its turn, Marx argued, the economic structure of capitalism with private ownership of the means of production and profit as a motivating force – hampers the full use of the growing productive forces and requires changes in property relations, and the substitution of social need for private profit, to permit unhampered use of the productive forces. And because these changes involve changes in the ownership of productive equipment, the contradiction between the conditions of production and the forces of production finds expression in antagonism between social groups, between those pressing for the retention of existing conditions of production in respect of property relations and those pressing for changes that will bring the conditions into correspondence with the productive forces. This antagonism between social groups, it is urged, provides the dynamic of social change; it is the class struggle.

It is important to do justice to this notion of class struggle in Marxist theory; for its part in this theory can be exaggerated as well as understated.

Classes are defined by Marx objectively in terms of property relations. Thus in any historical period the class owning the productive equipment of society, constitutes the economically ruling class. In an agrarian society, the economically dominant class is the landowning class; in an industrial society, the owners of factories, etc. The non-owning classes are therefore seen as dependent for their livelihoods on the owning classes and this relationship between owning and non-owning classes – privileged and non-privileged – constitutes an important factor in the general conditions in which production takes place.

Engels ascribed the emergence of class divisions within society to the growth of the productive forces to a level where a surplus beyond what was required for the elementary needs of life became possible. Primitive society, he supposed, was classless in structure because its level of production was so low that barely enough for all was produced. Hence, all had to share more or less equally in the task of obtaining the necessaries of life and all shared the results of collective effort. There was no room for a privileged class because there was no surplus to support it. To have had such a class in those circumstances would have meant exposing the group to loss of manpower through starvation of some of its members. Poverty, i.e., compelled equality.

Engels put it thus: 'As men emerged from the animal world – in the narrower sense of the word – so they made their entry into history; still half-animal, brutal, still helpless in face of the forces of nature, still ignorant of their own and consequently as poor as the animals and hardly more productive than those. There prevailed a certain equality in the conditions of existence and for the heads of families also a kind of social position – at least an absence of social classes.'[5]

This is the stage called by Engels *primitive communism*. Some anthropologists, however, notably Professor Malinowski, have denied that such a stage ever existed. Nevertheless, in his own study of the Trobriand Islanders, he instanced a number of practices which are reminiscent, at least, of a primitive communist phase. He described, e.g., the practices of communal labour as follows: 'Communal labour is an important factor in the tribal economy of the Trobriand natives. They resort to it in the building of living-huts and storehouses, in certain forms of industrial work, and in the transport of things, especially at harvest time, when great quantities of produce have to be shifted from one village to another, often over a great distance.'

It is interesting to note, too, that in his preface to Dr. Audrey I. Richard's study: *Hunger and Work in a Savage Tribe*, in which she stresses the basic communal character of food-getting in savage communities, Professor Malinowski wrote: 'And it is only now after I have become thoroughly acquainted with Dr. Richard's essay, that I see how much I missed in my own observations among the Melanesians. Were the present book only to force the field worker to keep his eyes and his mind open to the immense role which food plays in primitive societies, it would become a landmark in the history of anthropology.' Dr. Richards wrote: 'In most savage tribes starvation is a constant possibility if not an actual menace. The food quest is the chief occupation of every active member of the community and the most important institutions are concerned with the ownership and distribution of supplies.' Of the relation of the Basuto tribe to its grazing land, she wrote: 'according to native custom, the land occupied by a tribe is regarded theoretically as the property of the paramount chief: in relation to the tribe, he is a trustee, holding it for the people who occupy and use it, in subordination to him, on communist principles.' About the South-Eastern Bantu, she wrote: 'It owns grazing and

[5] *Anti-Dühring*, p. 206 (Martin Lawrence).

hunting ground in common ... Tribal as well as family and
household ties, depend on man's primary biological need for
food. As a member of his household group the child shared
and received food from certain individuals whom he recognised as members of his family and kinship group. As an
adult he reaches full economic status as a food producer
when he joins for the first time the great tribal activities, the
communal hunt, or the national ceremonies for first fruits
and rain.'

The conjecture that as man emerged from the animal
world in small family groups a condition of primitive communism prevailed is not, after all, so far-fetched. And the
need for constant food-getting activity on a co-operative basis
in the face of the ever-present menace of starvation would,
one would think, involve the kind of repression of mutual
jealousies that Engels posited in his *Origin of the Family*.

Experience, invention and discovery, stimulated by growing social units and consequent growing needs, brought a
measure of security and the possibility of a surplus, thereby
laying the foundations for a class division in society. Engels
conjectured that class divisions first arose with slavery. When
labour power was able to produce more than was necessary
for its own maintenance, additional labour forces would free
some members of society from complete involvement in the
work of society. Such forces, Engels suggested, were originally
provided by war. 'Up to that time they had not known what
to do with prisoners-of-war, and had therefore simply killed
them; at an earlier period eaten them. But at that stage of the
economic order which has now been attained, the prisoners
acquired a value; their captors therefore let them live and
made use of their labour; slavery was invented....'[6]

The division of society into classes corresponds, therefore,
with a definite stage of the development of the productive
forces, but since it establishes an inequality, expressed in
different shares in the wealth produced and differences in
privileges, it arouses antagonistic trends. So long as the class

[6] *Anti-Dühring*, p. 206.

divisions correspond with the needs of the productive process, so long, that is, as the productive process is not hampered by them and is allowed to expand, this antagonism is latent only. Indeed, wrote Engels: while 'the mode of production is in the rising stage of its development, it is enthusiastically welcomed even by those who come off worst from its corresponding mode of distribution.... When the conditions of its existence have to a large extent disappeared, and its successor is already knocking at the door – it is only at this stage that the constantly increasing inequality of distribution appears as unjust.'[7]

If we apply this to modern times, the main antagonism reflecting the contradiction between the growing forces of production and the conditions of production, is between the capitalist and working classes. The former performed an important historical role in bringing together the scattered instruments of production which previously existed. Before the present capitalist system, production was chiefly small-scale in character. The tools of production belonged to the producer, who, from his own raw material and by his own efforts, produced his commodities. The finished product was his by virtue of this fact. He owned the product of his labour. This petty form of industry became undermined towards the end of the fifteenth century, when trade and commerce received a mighty fillip from the discovery of America, the rounding of the Cape, the opening of the East Indian and Chinese markets, requiring a more extensive form of production. This necessitated the transformation of the scattered individual means of production into a form wherein they could be used by a number of workers co-operating in a productive process. 'The spinning wheel, the hand loom, and the blacksmith's hammer were replaced by the spinning machine, the mechanical loom, and the steam hammer; and the factory, making the co-operation of hundreds and thousands of workers necessary, took the place of the individual workroom. And, like the means of production, production itself

[7] *Anti-Dühring*, p. 170.

changed from a series of individual operations to a series of
social acts, and the products from the products of individuals
into social products.'[8]

In thus giving a social character to production, capitalism
performed an important historical task but it did so by
depriving the greater part of society of any ownership in the
means of production. The tools of the handicraftsmen were
rendered worthless in competition with the factory organisation of the capitalists, and the small masters were squeezed
out of existence. This process was particularly marked during
the Industrial Revolution in the second half of the eigh-
teenth century, with the invention of the steam-engine, spinning machines, the power loom, etc. Consequently a class of
people possessing no means of production, a class of prole-
tarians, came into being. 'The lower strata of the middle class
– the small tradespeople, shopkeepers, and retired tradesmen
generally, the handicraftsmen and peasants – all these sink
gradually into the proletariat, partly because their diminu-
tive capital does not suffice for the scale on which modern
industry is carried on and is swamped in the competition
with the large capitalists, partly because their special skill is
rendered worthless by the new methods of production. Thus
the proletariat is recruited from all classes of the population.'[9]

But while capitalist large-scale production introduces a
social basis to production, and while it organises and plans
production within the factory, it retains the individual
character of ownership which marked the petty production
that it superseded.

The purpose of production, in early mediaeval times, was
to satisfy the need of the producer and his family. He consumed his own product. Later an exchange took place between the artisan in the town and the peasant in the country,
the former selling his product to the latter and purchasing
agricultural goods. This type of exchange arose spontaneously
from the division of labour and had no plan of production

[8] *Anti-Dühring*, p. 302.
[9] *Communist Manifesto*.

guiding it. Each individual producer worked independently of the other producers, and was therefore in no position to gauge with any precision how much of his product was needed.

This planless character of production was carried over, together with individual ownership of the means of production, to the capitalist mode of production, but in a greatly accentuated form; because the planned production in the factory enabled vast masses of commodities to be produced, which were thrown on the market by each producing concern, independently of the other. 'The contradiction between social production and capitalist appropriation,' wrote Engels, 'reproduces itself as the antagonism between the organisation of production in the individual factory and the anarchy of production in society as a whole.'

It is within this framework of contrast between social production and private ownership, between plan within the factory and planlessness within society, that the Marxist analysis of the tendencies of capitalism was made. Forecasts about the future of social trends are bound to have a large speculative element in them. A trend that may seem strong at one time may be diverted or halted by other factors unsuspected at the time the trend was strong. Both the first and second world wars gave tremendous fillips to invention and discovery and transformed productive techniques. The strengthening of workers' movements, their trades unions and labour organisations, enabled the working class to gain larger shares of the social product and to reverse, to some degree, the process of impoverishment that seemed continuous to Marx. These were factors- that Marx could not completely foresee, certainly not in detail. As a consequence it has sometimes been claimed that Marx has been refuted. The simple, relatively clearcut line of development which he predicted on the basis of his analysis has not happened. Therefore, it is argued, the analysis is faulty.[10]

[10] As a matter of fact, Marx was well aware that there may be modifying factors. He was concerned to state, in a general form, the laws of capitalist development. Thus he wrote: 'Like all other laws, it is modified in its actual working by numerous considerations.' *Capital*, p. 712.

In particular, the work of Keynes and Galbraith are quoted in refutation of Marxism. But both these writers place great emphasis on Government intervention in economic life, an intervention that, to some extent, suspends the profit motive in determining spheres of capital investment.

But this is no more a refutation of Marxism than the aeroplane, as a conscious intervention in physical laws, is a refutation of gravitation. The point of the Marxist economic analysis is that private control of capital plus the profit motive lead to anarchy in production and distribution.

It is, of course, possible to think up ways of mitigating the anarchic effects of capitalist production, and economists who are, no doubt, familiar with the Marxist analysis may well supply Governments with schemes of public investment and so forth, that aim to introduce some rationality into the economic life of capitalism. If governments could be induced to apply these schemes on such a scale as to offset the profit motive over a large field and give priority to social welfare, what would then be refuted would not be the Marxist economic analysis but its associated views about the selfishness and social irresponsibility of capitalists. In other words, the behavioural predictions of Marxism concerning capitalists, but not its economic analysis of capitalism, would be refuted. Keynes, Galbraith and their followers are really asking us to believe that the economic and political leaders of capitalism are less selfish and more rational than Marxists hold. I shall return to the claims that Marxism has been refuted from a more general standpoint, in the final chapter of this book.

Our account of Marxism so far has been limited to what Marx called the economic basis of society, namely the productive forces of society and the relationships among men within which these forces grow. We now turn to consider the 'ideological structure' that develops on this basis. And this brings us to the Marxist view of the relationship of men's thinking to their social environment, to the conditioning effect of this environment of their consciousness.

The classic formulation of the relationship of the superstructure to the economic base is contained in a passage in the *Critique of Political Economy* by Marx. The passage begins with the point already made above, namely, that, in the productive process men enter into relations of production corresponding to a definite stage of development of the productive forces, and continues: 'The sum total of these relations of production constitutes the economic structure of society – the real foundation on which rises a legal and political superstructure and to which correspond definite forms of social consciousness. *The mode of production in material life conditions the social, political and intellectual life process in general.* It is not the consciousness of men that determines their being, but, on the contrary, their social being that determines their consciousness. At a certain stage of their development the material forces of production in society come in conflict with the existing relations of production, or – what is but a legal expression for the same thing – with the property relations within which they have been at work before. From forms of development of the forces of production these relations turn into their fetters. Then begins an epoch of social revolution. With the change of the economic foundation the entire immense superstructure is more or less rapidly transformed. In considering such transformations a distinction should always be made between the material transformation of the economic conditions of production, which can be determined with the precision of natural science, and the legal, political, religious, aesthetic or philosophic – in short, ideological forms in which men become conscious of this conflict and fight it out.'

This highly concentrated statement of historical materialism turns very much upon the sense in which Marx uses such terms as 'determine' and 'condition'. The widest sense in which the material base may be said to determine or condition the superstructure is expressed in the following words of Engels at the grave of Marx. 'Just as Darwin discovered the law of development of organic nature, so Marx discovered the law of development of human history; the simple fact, hitherto concealed by an overgrowth of ideology, that mankind must first of all eat, drink, and have shelter and clothing, before it can pursue politics, science, art, religion etc.'

In other words, a certain level of material production is required before there can be any development of cultural life. A society must be able to afford to allow some of its members to spend time in non-productive activities; it must, that is to say, be in a position to produce a surplus upon which they can live. This was recognised by Aristotle who saw that leisure for some was a prerequisite for the development of the cultural life of society. The slavery of Greek society, as Engels pointed out in *Anti-Dühring* provided the material basis for the flowering of Greek art, science and philosophy. In this broad sense, to say that the material level of production determines the growth of intellectual life is to say that it sets the bounds or limits within which intellectual life may grow; to some extent it sets the kind of problems with which intellectual life may concern itself. The relation between the material level of production and intellectual life may, in this sense, be expressed in the truism that artists, scientists, philosophers, must have the means to eat, drink and be housed, if they are to make their contributions to the life of society.

But, I think, Marx meant much more than this. He was not simply concerned to say that a certain level of material life is necessary for any cultural life to develop. He was concerned to say that the *kind* of culture which develops bears an important relation to the *kind* of society, with its specific class structure, in which it develops. It is in this sense, in particular, that Marx used the term 'determine'.

In a general sense, culture – men's interest in art, literature, music, science, philosophy – is a specifically human form of activity, possible, at least on a large scale, only when men have achieved a level of production which frees some of them from the need for fulltime participation in the productive process. In the special sense, in which the kind of culture will be determined by the kind of society, literature, art, politics,

science, philosophy, religion, will be ideologically slanted so
as to reflect and protect the interests of a ruling class. There
is, that is to say, a certain appropriateness between the ideas
current at any time and the interests of dominant groups.
These ideas may cast a protective facade over the interests of
the dominant groups so that the special interests of the
groups are represented as the general interests of society. This
kind of process was well described by Hume in his essay on
the 'Original Contract'. He wrote: 'As no party, in the
present age, can well support itself without a philosophical or
speculative system of principles annexed to its political or
practical one, we accordingly find that each of the factions
into which this nation is divided has reared up a fabric of the
former kind, in order to protect and cover that scheme of
actions which it pursues ... the one party, by tracing up
government to the Deity, to render it so sacred and inviolate,
that it must be little less than sacrilege, however tyrannical it
may become, to touch or invade it in the smallest article.

'The other party, by founding government altogether on
the consent of the people, suppose that there is a kind of
original contract, by which the subjects have tacitly reserved
the power of resisting their sovereign, whenever they find
themselves aggrieved by that authority, with which they
have, for certain purposes, voluntarily entrusted him. These
are the speculative principles of the two parties, and these,
too, are the practical consequences deduced from them.'

This view of Marx, that culture is ideologically slanted to
justify class interests, accords well with the Freudian concept
of *rationalisation*. Indeed, Engels described the process in
terms which are startlingly modern and might have been
written by a psycho-analyst. Thus he wrote: 'Ideology is a
process accomplished by the so-called thinker consciously,
indeed, but with a false consciousness. The real motives impelling him remain unknown to him, otherwise it would not
be an ideological process at all. Hence he imagines false or
apparent motives.'

What Freud has discovered in the individual psyche, Marx

discovered in the wider network of human relations, in society.

It is important to note that the fact that aspects of men's cultural life can be used to justify particular economic interests, does not necessarily imply that these aspects have no meaning except in terms of these economic interests. There is an important distinction between the questions: 'in what circumstances did a particular viewpoint develop and what function does it play in social life' and the question 'is the viewpoint true or valid'. Thus one may ask for an account of the circumstances which gave an impetus to Darwinian theory and note that it has sometimes been presented as a justification for the emergence of rich, powerful groups in society. This is to note the ideological use which has been made of it. But there still remains the question concerning the adequacy of the theory to account for the facts in its field of inquiry – the question: 'is the theory true or false?' If this were not so, it would place Marxist theory itself in a para-doxical situation. It would mean that Marxism, as the pro-duct of certain historical conditions and as a theoretical weapon in the hands of the working class, had no more claim to be true than any other theoretical system purporting to account for historical change. It would simply be the product of different conditions, serving different class interests. And this is certainly not what Marx intended to say.

In short, we need to distinguish between the ideological form of a theory – the fact that it can be used to support and justify certain social interests – and its adequacy as a theory to account for the facts to which it relates or to supply an answer to the problem with which it is concerned.

To return to a general consideration of Marx's historical theory. It is best seen, I think, not as a formula rigidly stating the relations between an ideological superstructure and a material base, but as a way of approach to social study, a means of investigating the structure of society in terms of its productive technique. Engels put the matter clearly in these terms. 'But our conception of history is above all *a guide to study*, not a lever for construction *à la Hegelianism*. All history must be studied afresh, the conditions of existence of the different formations of society must be examined in detail' ... He went on to admonish the Marxists who, he said, 'make use of the phrase historical materialism ... only in order to get their own relatively scanty historical knowledge ... constructed into a neat system as quickly as possible, and then they think themselves something very tremendous'.

Thus Marxist historical theory stresses that a consideration of the productive methods by which people get their livings, an examination of the productive relations, the class stratifications, the property relations, may supply a leading thread in the tangled drama of history. Few contemporary historians would deny the value of this way of looking at history. Professor Butterfield, e.g. in a critical survey of Marx's theory of history wrote: 'The Marxian formula defines a method, provides a clue for a person who wishes to construct a survey of general history, or to discuss some historical research. It is the definition of the predisposition which we should bring when we come to the study of history, and neither this nor any other interpretation of its kind can validly provide us with anything more. This point has been greatly stressed by modern exponents of the theory. In other words, where we should in any case act upon one assumption or another, the Marxian formula prescribes a way of approach; it tells us which end of the stick to pick up.'[11]

What bearing has Freudian theory on this Marxist stress on the conditioning impact of man's economic and social life? The ego, in Freudian terminology, is that part of the id which has been modified by external reality, an external reality which is largely, for man, economic and social. The ego, in other words, mirrors social reality and the ego is compelled to limit and restrain the demands of the id in conformity with the exigencies of social reality. Marx said that

[11] H. Butterfield: *History and the Marxian Method—Scrutiny*, Vol. I, No. 4, 1933, p. 344.

man's consciousness is determined by his social existence, a general statement with which Freudian theory must agree. But the Freudians go further and point out that the relationship between the conscious ego and the external social world is not one-sided, not a passive relationship of the ego to the world, but one in which the ego seeks actively for forms of expression of id impulses. The ego, in other words, does not only mirror reality for the id, but strives to reshape reality the better to serve the ends of the id. In this way, Freudian theory enriches the bare Marxist dictum about social reality determining consciousness. It says, in effect, that we must not only study social reality as a determining influence on consciousness but must also study the psychological processes which give content to consciousness, which impel and motivate it to reach out to external reality. In chapter four we saw something of the psychological processes through which the ego mediates between external reality and the id, how through projection, sublimation, rationalisation, the ego deals with id impulses and reconciles their demands with those of external reality. What is true of the individual psyche in relation to the world seems to be true on the larger scale of social groups within society. The ruling class, we saw, rationalises its interests so that they appear to be the interests of society as a whole. It erects a complex ideological structure of philosophical, religious, political arguments in favour of its own retention of power and privilege.

But there is more to it than this. For the ego has not only the task of mediating between the id and reality. It is saddled with the super-ego, the outgrowth of authority as perceived by the weak, uncritical ego of childhood. The ego, as Freud put it, has to serve two masters and to the super-ego is due the irrational influence of tradition and often outworn authority in the lives of men.

Let us remind ourselves of the circumstances in which the super-ego is formed so that we can better evaluate the part it plays in social life.

The child's first taste of reality, its first rebuffs and grati-

fications, come largely from those most closely related to it –
its parents, friends, etc. Helplessness for a long time is an
important biological characteristic of human beings which
exists and would exist under any social system. The psychological reaction of the child to this helplessness, this almost
complete dependence upon adults is bound to have common
features in any social milieu, as inevitable as the helplessness
itself.

The child comes to recognise some external authority as
having the power to curtail the satisfaction of its needs. In a
myriad of ways the child is made to feel the essential difference between it and the adult, in the ability of the latter to
satisfy, or to prevent satisfaction of, its needs. The role that
the parents, or other authorities, have played in exacting
from the child adjustment to the demands of external reality,
leaves its mark on the child. While the ego is yet weak, and
unable to control the imperative demands of the id, a portion
of the ego becomes identified with the parent, and, in the
form of the super-ego, continues to watch over the id impulses, compelling the ego to repress those it deems impermissible. In later life, this super-ego surveillance compels
obeisance to authorities external to the individual and is
particularly responsible for the uncritical nature of the
adult's acceptance of the authority of church, state, political
party and so forth. In this sense, the super-ego explains the
irrational conservatism that leads to the perpetuation of outworn social systems. Social reformers are well aware that their
strongest opposition comes from the dead weight of tradition,
the emotional bondage to existing social institutions. Such
institutions cannot be understood without knowledge of the
part that the super-ego plays in their life. For while their
character may be due, in large part, to economic and social
necessity, the authority that they acquire over men's actions
and which they often retain long after their raison d'être has
disappeared, is due to the compulsions of the super-ego.

The super-ego, then, is the means of handing down traditional modes of behaviour. As Freud put it 'Mankind never

completely lives in the present; the ideologies of the super-ego perpetuate the past, the traditions of the race and people, which yields but slowly to the influence of the present and to new developments of economic conditions.'

Marxism has pointed out how traditions, institutions, ideologies, come to serve the interests of ruling sections in society. But it does not explain the uncritical allegiance to them of people in whose interest they do not work. This important explanatory task is performed by the Freudian theory of the super-ego. If it were not for the compulsions of the super-ego, the task of social reformers would be immeasurably easier. It would only be necessary to explain how certain social changes would reduce social evils and benefit the people as a whole. If rational explanations had not to meet the resistance inspired by super-ego attachment to outworn social institutions, men would quickly become aware of the need to bring social institutions into correspondence with economic reality.

For this reason those psycho-analysts who turn their attention to social problems and see the need for a social change, regard the essential task as the substitution of 'ego morality' for 'super-ego morality'. Professor Flugel, for example, saw the aim of 'progressive sociology' as the strengthening of the ego as against the 'crude and more unconscious control of the super-ego', which means freeing the individual from reliance on irrational authority and enabling his rational side to gain greater control over his personality.

The social reformer, I think, can turn to Marxism for light on the economic and, in general, historical causes of the social evils of today. He seeks to get people to act and think in a rational manner, a manner that takes cognizance of the realities of social life. But he can hardly hope to give this rational direction to behaviour if he leaves unanswered basic questions concerning the source of much of man's irrationality. If, on the other hand, he is armed with a knowledge of the unconscious motivations of human behaviour, he is better able to give these unconscious forces an objective, rational direction.

8

Dialectical Materialism

Freud and Marx belong to that class of great thinkers whose theories compel us to look afresh, not only at the problems in the immediate field of their enquiries, but over the whole range of problems stemming from human existence. For both Freud and Marx philosophy was essentially a quest for a world outlook, a *weltanschauung*, but whereas Freud regarded psycho-analysis as contributing to the scientific weltanschauung, Marxism aims at a comprehensive view of the universe and man's place in it, utilising both common human experience and the findings of science to this end.

Marxists have tended to regard the contributions of Freud with suspicion. They have not fitted in easily with the picture that Marxist theorists have drawn largely from material from the physical sciences, from biological, social and political studies. Nevertheless, as I hope to show in this chapter, there is much in Freudian theory that blends well with this Marxist picture and much that enriches, and corrects, some of its cruder aspects. I shall begin with an outline of the main features of Marxist philosophy, the philosophy of dialectical materialism. I shall then try to show how Freudian theory stands in relation to this philosophy.

It is necessary to stress, at the outset, that materialism as used in dialectical materialism is quite different, in meaning, from materialism as used in a popular, and often, derogatory sense. In the latter sense, materialism often means self-interest, contempt for culture, grossness and so forth. In the Marxist sense, materialism is the view that the external world has an independent existence of its own. It does not depend for its existence on our minds or any minds. It is, indeed, the ordinary, everyday assumption that there is an external world; that trees, mountains, houses, other people, exist in their own right, that gives a foundation for materialist philosophy.

On the other hand, idealism, as used by Marxists, has nothing to do with ideals. It would be more correctly termed idea-ism, or mentalism, in Marxist usage. For it is a general term, applied by Marxists to any philosophic tendency that raises doubts about the independent existence of the external world. It applies the term, e.g., to the Kantian view that the spacetime qualities which the world appears to have in its own right, are, in fact, projected upon the world by our minds, as well as to the more sweeping assertion of Berkeley that material objects have an existence only as perceptions in our or God's mind. Any philosophical view that falls short of a forthright assertion of the independent existence of the external world and the dependent, derivative nature of mental life, is dubbed by Marxists 'idealistic'.

Marxists regard idealism as a socially harmful viewpoint. They argue that if we regard the external world as somehow not quite real or independent, we shall be tempted to treat its problems as not quite real. We shall deny that science gives us any real knowledge or power; for in wrestling with an external world which, in some measure, is a projection of our own minds, we are wrestling with a shadow world. Hence, it is argued, idealism encourages a tendency to turn from the pressing social problems needing our attention. On the other hand, the belief in the independent existence of the world acts as a spur to scientific discovery. Nature is a challenge just because it exists independently of our wills, presenting obstacles to be overcome. It makes sense, also, of the knowledge supplied by geology, astronomy and other sciences. For these tell us that the universe existed for millions of years before life emerged. Consciousness is a late comer in the universe appearing when living matter had reached a high degree of complexity.

The defence of materialism is, therefore, largely an appeal to common everyday experience and scientific knowledge. Ontologically, Marxism takes its stand firmly on science and common sense.

But this is only the beginning of Marxist philosophy. It calls itself *dialectical* materialism because it claims that the universe exhibits certain dynamic patterns of change and growth which may be summed up in the *dialectical* laws of change. Marx adopted the terminology of Hegel to describe his views largely as a gesture in Hegel's honour. He wrote: 'Nearly thirty years ago, when Hegelianism was still fashionable, I criticised the mystifying aspect of the Hegelian dialectic. But at the very time I was working at the first volume of *Das Kapital*, the peevish and arrogant mediocrities who nowadays have the ear of the educated public in Germany, were fond of treating Hegel much as in Lessing's day the world of Moses Mendelssohn used to treat Spinoza, namely, as a "dead dog". That was why I frankly proclaimed myself a disciple of that great thinker, and even, in *Das Kapital*, toyed with the use of Hegelian terminology, when discussing the theory of value.'[1] Marx has often been criticised for his use of Hegelian terminology on the grounds that the so-called dialectical laws exhibit the mystification that Marx claimed to have expelled from Hegelianism. But while the Hegelian terminology does seem somewhat odd we shall see that the use Marx made of it relates to some highly important processes both in the external world and human thinking.

Let us say something first about the background of the dialectical view.

The dialectical view of reality received its main impetus in

[1] Preface to the Second Edition of *Capital*.

the nineteenth century, when the view that the world was the product of a long process of evolution was making its way. The old Greek logic which dealt with rigid, unchanging things was felt to be inadequate to deal with the changing rhythm of the universe. Aristotle had formulated three laws which gave a framework for reasoning about all things and which had remained almost completely unchallenged to the beginning of the nineteenth century.

The first of his laws establishes the identity of whatever is under consideration. It marks it out from the rest of the universe, stating that A is A, with its own distinct and peculiar properties. Hence it was called the Law of Identity. The second law, the Law of Contradiction, states that A is *only* A and nothing else – it is not B. In the third law, the Law of the Excluded Middle Term, this is emphasised by stating that between A and B there is no middle term. Contradiction is thus excluded and the objects of the world are treated as rigidly separate and created in a fixed pattern.

But in face of the growing knowledge that the higher and more complex forms of existence are related to the lower and more simple; that what had been considered the result of a divine act of creation, was really the result of a lengthy process of evolution, there arose a need for a logic which expressed these facts.

In the nineteenth century Hegel elaborated a logic which was more in keeping with the evolutionary outlook then making its way.

He called his method of logic the dialectic, after the Greek expression, meaning the art of discussion in which, by refutation and clash of opinion, a synthesis of the contradictory views takes place, approaching nearer the truth.

Hegel saw in the struggle of contradictory elements the real cause of all developmental change. All things, he argued, are in process of becoming something else, are in a constant state of flux, which makes the logical categories of Aristotle inadequate to contain them. A is A, it is true, but it is also becoming not-A. It is not sharply separated from the rest of the universe but closely related to it. In developing contradictory aspects it passes into new forms of being.

The objects in which the contradiction is working Hegel termed the *positive*. The contradiction, he termed the *negative;* and the reconciliation of the contradiction in a new synthesis, he termed the *negation of the negation*.

The whole process was represented as thesis, antithesis and synthesis in which the latter denoted the raising of the process to a new stage of development.

Hegel, however, was an idealist (in the Marxist sense of this word). He saw the whole evolutionary process as the unfolding of the Idea or Absolute Spirit which existed eternally.

The material world was seen by Hegel as the creation of this Idea, and the evolution of this world manifested, for him, the stages by which the Idea revealed itself.

The process of struggle and contradiction in the real world revealed the absolute idea stage by stage, and as each stage became obsolete because of the maturity of contradictions it became unreal. For Hegel the unreal was also the unreasonable, for it contradicted the necessities of the Absolute Idea. 'That which is real,' he wrote, 'is reasonable, and that which is reasonable is real.'

Among the students of Hegel, a group developed called the Young Hegelians who opposed the conservative use to which Hegelian philosophy was being put. Using Hegel's dictum that what was real was reasonable, the advocates of the Prussian government of the time, found justification for its existence. It was real, therefore reasonable. The best possible government for the time.

This, as Engels showed in his book on Feuerbach, was a distortion of Hegel's meaning; for it is not the actual existence of a thing which gives it reality, in the Hegelian sense, but the necessity for it. If it had become obsolete and therefore unnecessary, it had also become unreal.

Marx used the Hegelian dialectic to understand the real world, the world existing independently of thought. His use of the dialectic was, in his own words, the direct opposite of

Hegel's. 'For Hegel,' he wrote, 'the thought process (which he actually transforms into an independent subject, giving it the name of "Idea") is the creator of the real; and for him the real is only the outward manifestation of the idea. In my view, on the other hand, the idea is nothing other than the material when it has been transposed and translated inside the human head. . . . In Hegel's writings dialectic stands on its head. You must turn it right way up again if you want to discover the rational kernel is hidden away with the wrappings of mystification.'

Marx nowhere developed fully his dialectical view of reality. In his own words, he 'toyed' with the use of Hegelian terminology in his major literary work. His co-worker Engels and later Marxists have given fuller accounts of the Marxist dialectics upon which the following summary is largely based.

To begin with, dialectical materialism stresses the changing nature of reality. 'All nature,' wrote Engels, 'from the smallest thing to the biggest, from a grain of sand to the sun . . . is in constant state of coming into being and going out of being, in a constant flux, in a ceaseless state of movement and change.' It further stresses the inter-relationship of all things. Nothing, it says, can be understood by itself alone. It must be seen in its relationship with other things. Naturally, some relationships are more important than others and it is the task of science to distinguish the relevant relationships from the irrelevant in any particular sphere of study. To see things in terms of movement and change, in their relationships with other things, is, then, the first principle of dialectical thinking. The special sciences are concerned with special kinds of changes within their fields of research. Dialectical materialism may be described as the study of the general character of change, manifested in the special fields of scientific research. In this changing character of reality, three main trends are discerned, referred to in dialectical materialism as the universal laws of change.

In characterising these laws Marx, and later Marxists, retained the terminology of Hegel. But one should not be misled by the queer Hegelian terminology. For, as the following account will try to show, these laws are very largely generalisations of the particular kinds of changes observed both in scientific research and everyday life. Shorn of their Hegelian garb, they stand out as reasonable summaries of the kind of changes that take place in the world and the direction and consequences of these changes. These laws, then, are (1) the law of the transformation of quantity into quality; (2) the law of the unity of opposites, and (3) the law of the negation of the negation. I propose to outline them briefly. It should be stressed that these laws are closely inter-dependent and can only be considered separately for purposes of exposition.

The law of the transformation of quantity into quality is concerned with the myriad variety of changes taking place in the universe. It summarises these changes as of two kinds, quantitative and qualitative. A quantitative change takes place, e.g., if we add more sand to an existing pile of sand. The sand remains sand, with its distinctive qualities but there is more of it. We need no new descriptive terms for it. But there are changes that take place in which new qualities appear, which require new terms to describe them, which add something to the changing object that cannot be stated in numerical terms. Now there is often discernible an important relationship between these latter qualitative changes and the former quantitative ones. It seems that the qualitative changes make their appearance following a process of quantitative change; that, as it were, quantitative change itself changes into qualitative change. There seems to be a continuous accumulation of quantitative change and then the continuity is broken and a new quality or qualities emerges. A familiar example, often quoted but none-the-less strikingly illustrating this quantity-quality process, is provided in the freezing of water. When water is subjected to a quantitative change in temperature it becomes ice. It does not become increasingly pulpy until it assumes the rigidity of ice but changes suddenly when the critical temperature is reached. The normal process of growth involves qualitative change following quantitative change. An oak tree grows from a small acorn but it is not merely a large acorn. In growth it has developed new qualities. And the same is true of the human being. He begins life as the fusion of two cells which grow quantitatively and qualitatively. The important fact about qualities which arise, or emerge, from preceding quantitative changes is that they cannot be reduced to, or expressed in terms of, the preceding quantitative changes. Something is involved, something not wholly predictable from a considera-tion of the quantitative changes. This is a fact of observation made in every field of scientific research.

The meaning of the quantity-quality law is not difficult to grasp. It is a general statement concerning the kind of rela-tion between the two kinds of change discernible in every department of reality. It does not necessarily imply that all quantitative changes will give rise to qualitative changes within any measurable period. In some cases, quantitative changes may seem to extend for indefinite periods. This is true of the changes that have taken place in the development of the solar system. Nor can we assert with certainty that all quantitative changes inevitably give rise to qualitative changes. We can only point to the frequent relationship of quantitative-quality change as the basis for a generalisation, that quantitative changes tend to lead to qualitative changes and that the latter are not reducible to the former. This law is sometimes known as the theory of emergent changes and few scientists today would deny that such changes do take place. Attempts are sometimes made to explain new quali-ties entirely in terms of preceding quantitative changes but they have generally failed. In psychology, e.g. it has been hoped that mental processes could be adequately explained in terms of their underlying physiological processes but the most ambitious of these attempts have failed. Clark C. Hull and E. C. Tolman, two leading American behaviourists, e.g., have acknowledged that the 'gap between the minute ana-tomical and physiological account of the nervous system as at present known and what would be required for the construction of a reasonably adequate theory of molar behaviour is impassable' (Hull). Tolman stressed the existence of this gap in these words: 'Behaviour, as such, is an "emergent" phenomenon that has descriptive and defining properties of its own.'

The quantity-quality law, then, is widely accepted as a sound generalisation far beyond Marxist circles and one might term it a quite respectable, unexciting generalisation confirmed in many spheres of scientific research. But the law related to it, the Law of the Unity of Opposites, is on a different footing. For it attempts to account for the dynamics of quantity-quality change, in terms of the Hegelian notion of contradiction and struggle, of interpenetration of opposites within a changing process. It states that everything that can be observed is an unstable unity of opposing factors, of positive and negative processes. Some of these factors make for the conservation of the object in its existing form, others make for its transformation into something new. From these conflicting forces an inner movement results beginning on a quantitative level and rising to a qualitative level. This law is bound up with the view of things as essentially processes, coming into being and passing into new forms of existence.

Like the quantity-quality law, the law of the unity of opposites has an obvious common-sense aspect, supported by innumerable examples from science. Thus we know that structurally the physical world exhibits a fluctuating equilibrium of opposing forces in all its forms, down to the minutest combination of electrical particles. The life processes of the body depend upon opposing processes, the anabolic building-up processes and the katabolic, breaking-down processes. The simplest movement of the body involves an opposition of flexor and tensor muscles.

What gives dialectical materialism its special interest is its emphasis upon the part played by opposition, or contradiction as it terms it, in developmental change. It sees the unity of opposites as something more than a juxtaposition of opposing factors but as an opposition leading to movement and change. It speaks of the inner movement of processes resulting from the inner contradictions. It instances, e.g. the evolutionary process which led to the emergence of life on the earth. Thus at one time the solar system was a flaming mass of gas but the contrary processes of cooling and condensation in one part of the solar system established conditions that led to the appearance of living organisms. But it is in relation to social development that the law of the unity of opposites shows itself most strikingly. History is regarded by Marxists, as we have seen, as a progressive movement resulting from the conflict between the forces of production and the conditions of production. Engels described this process as follows: 'All civilised peoples begin with the common ownership of the land. With all peoples who have passed a certain primitive stage in the course of the development of agriculture this common ownership becomes a fetter on production. It is abolished, negated, and, after a longer or shorter series of intermediate stages, is transformed into private property. But at a higher stage of agricultural development, brought about by private ownership in land itself, private property in turn becomes a fetter on production, as is the case today, both with small and large landownership. The demand that it also should be negated, that it should once again be transformed into common property, necessarily arises. But this demand does not mean the restoration of the old original ownership, but the institution of a far higher and more developed form of possession in common which, far from being a hindrance to production, on the contrary for the first time frees production from all fetters and gives it the possibility of making full use of modern chemical discoveries and mechanical inventions.'[2]

In other words, the original state of common ownership is negated by private property – a transformation, that is to say, of common ownership into its opposite, private property. But private property becoming a fetter on production in its turn, becomes transformed into *its* opposite, common property – that is, a return to the original status, but on a higher

[2] *Anti-Dühring*, pp. 156-7.

level. Private property, the negation, itself suffers negation.

This process illustrates the third of the dialectical laws, the *negation of the negation*. And this means, not a mere cancelling of a state of affairs, but the realisation, through struggle, of a higher stage of development, the reaching of a new synthesis in which new contradictions will emerge leading to further development. An excellent description of this process as exemplified in biological development appears in J. Z. Young's *Reith Lectures* for 1950. He wrote: 'Each species remains in balance with its surroundings by alternative periods of development and death, followed by replacement by a new version of the organisation. This is the means by which life maintains, as it were, communication with the non-living world.'[3]

These, then, are the dialectical laws of development. If we restate the dialectical view without its Hegelian terminology it comes roughly to this: that there is a world outside us: that it is subject to change: that this change is sometimes smooth and continuous, sometimes sudden; that new qualities emerge from quantitative change; that organisms and societies grow through inner tensions which are resolved in new states of equilibrium. These are generalisations which find considerable support in many, if not every, field of scientific enquiry. Properly used, they form an excellent background for any scientific research. The researcher is safeguarded against the temptation to consider his field of enquiry in complete detachment from other fields of enquiry. He is reminded, when considering a process undergoing change, to look for contradictory factors, to be prepared for the emergence of new qualities. This aspect of Marxism, its ontological scheme, fits in well with the temper of scientific thought.

Let us now see how psycho-analysis fits in with this dialectical view.

[3] J. Z. Young, *Doubt and Certainty in Science,* p. 161.

In the first place, it offers a view of mental life as an interplay of urging and repressing forces, with conflict as a central dynamic factor. Mental life is thus seen as a unity of opposing forces, conscious and unconscious elements from whose interaction are born the richness and variety of man's thoughts and feelings. Freud's notions of the relations of id, ego, superego and external world, are shot through and through with dialectical implications. The id impulses, e.g., are transformed into their opposite, the ego, as a consequence of conflict with external reality. The ego is rational where the id is irrational; logical where the id is illogical; has a reality principle where the id seeks gratification on a pleasure principle. The ego, in other words, represents a true qualitative development.

Further the id is viewed as combining two opposing instinctive groups – Eros, or life instincts and Death, or destructive instincts – whose fusion forms part of every instinctive activity. The death instincts, said Freud, seek the reinstatement of an inanimate state of affairs, while the life instincts strive to build up and preserve the organism. Life is seen as a process involving the struggle between building-up and breaking-down processes, a fact stated by Engels as follows: 'Every organic being is at each moment the same and not the same; at each moment it is assimilating matter drawn from without, and excreting other matter; at each moment the cells of the body are dying and new ones are being formed.'[4] This purely physiological account of the birth and death of cells can well be interpreted as the basis from which develops the complex notion of life and death instincts.

Another important Freudian concept with striking dialectical implications is repression. This is a process set up in the mind through the conflict of reality with the demands of the id. It is repression which, in the Freudian scheme, compels the transformation of unconscious impulses into the more socially acceptable conscious modes of behaviour. The

[4] *Anti-Dühring*, p. 29 (Martin Lawrence).

displacements, sublimations, reaction-formations which we discussed in chapter four are qualitative transformations of id impulses, occurring when repression has reached a certain critical intensity. Freud described the quantity-quality relation between the conflicting forces as follows: 'You will have noticed ... I have introduced a new factor into the concatenation of the aetiological chain – namely, the *quantity*, the magnitude of the energies concerned; we must always take this factor into account as well. A purely qualitative analysis of the aetiological conditions does not suffice ... we have to realise that the conflict between the two forces in opposition does not break out until a certain intensity in the degree of investment is reached ... no less important is this quantitative factor for the capacity to withstand neurotic illness; it depends upon the *amount* of undischarged libido that a person can hold freely suspended, and upon *how large* a portion of it he can deflect from the sexual to a non-sexual goal in sublimation.'[5]

If we turn to Freud's theory of dream-life, the dialectical character of Freudian theory is again well illustrated.

In dreams, according to Freud, the repressed desires gain a measure of expression denied them in waking life. In this sense, dream-life is the opposite, the Hegelian *other* of waking life. Its form of mental presentation is the opposite of that of waking life. In the latter, thought is general, ideas are formed through abstraction from the concrete. The concrete is perceived in terms of the abstract, whereas in dreams abstract ideas are presented in concrete form.

The way of dealing with experiences by abstracting general qualities carries the tendency to render in static form what is really in motion. Dream-life, on the other hand, presents its contents in a form of highly dramatised action. In waking life, things are considered apart and distinct from one another. Dream-life, on the other hand, seems to reflect more closely, although often in a bizarre way, the interconnections among things for it quite readily uses one thing to symbolise

[5] *Introductory Lectures*, p. 313.

another which, in waking life, may seem to have no connection. It can combine the most contradictory elements in
one. As Freud wrote: 'One of our most surprising discoveries
is the manner in which *opposites* in the latent dream are
dealt with by the dream-work ... Now contraries are treated
in just the same way as similarities, with a marked preference
for expression by means of the same manifest element. An
element in the manifest dream which admits of an opposite
may stand simply for itself, or for its opposite, or for both
together.'[6]

In a curious way, it seems as if dream-life is in closer touch
with the dynamic nature of reality than is waking life. For
consciousness tends to represent the process in the external
world as rigid and distinct. This was recognised by Engels
who wrote of the 'imagined rigidity and absoluteness (of the
distinctions found in Nature) as having been introduced into
Nature only by our minds'. Here indeed is a poser for the
dialectician. For it argues that the thinking process by which
reality is reflected to consciousness, distorts the dialectical
nature of reality, presenting it in highly undialectical terms.
The Freudian answer to this poser, I think, would be to point
to the tendency of the ego, confronted with the demands of
the id, to exaggerate the harshness of reality to the id. It
might be argued that just as to the ego the image of the father
tends to assume harsh and uncompromising shape in the form
of the super-ego, so reality, too, tends to assume 'an imagined
rigidity and absoluteness' to the ego, and the repression of id
impulses thereby strengthened. Indeed, we can go on, with
this Freudian explanation, and relate the growing evolutionary, and dialectical, view of reality to the conquests man has
made in his natural environment. Nature no longer seems so
intractable, and consequently its representation by the ego
tends to be less rigid.

We turn now from the problem of the nature of external
reality, as seen through Marxist and Freudian eyes, to the
problem of the validity of our knowledge of the external

[6] *Introductory Lectures*, p. 150.

world. In philosophical terms, we turn from ontological considerations to those of epistemology, of Theory of Knowledge. It will be necessary to sketch in the background of philosophic controversy concerning our knowledge of the external world if the Marxist and Freudian views are to be seen in correct perspective.

Since Plato, philosophers have raised doubts about the reliability of the information about the world supplied by our senses. The world as presented to us through our senses, he called the *sensible* world and he challenged its reliability on two main grounds. In the first place, he pointed out that we can have no definite knowledge of the sensible world because it has no definite qualities which may be known. All we have are conflicting beliefs or opinions relative to the viewpoint of the observer. For example, if after my hand has been frozen in a blizzard, I put it into a bucket of lukewarm water, I shall declare the water to be cold. Is the water, then, both hot and cold? Again I call a rabbit large in comparison with a fly. Is it then both large and small?

Plato's answer was that a thing could not have contradictory qualities. If it was large, it clearly was not small. Hence these contradictory qualities could not be said to belong to the object itself. Rather the object fluctuated between these qualities, appearing to have one or the other according to the viewpoint of the observer. This, he maintained, was true of all objects in the sensible world. Their qualities are relative to the observer, are expressions of his opinion or belief, rather than definite qualities possessed by objects.

But, Plato's argument continues, if a thing has no definite qualities it cannot be said to have real existence. For what is real must also, he contended, be knowable. Hence the world of sensible objects that we see around us can have no full reality. At best it has only a kind of semi-reality.

Moreover, said Plato, there is nothing in the sensible world sufficiently stable to form the object of definite knowledge. For nothing remains itself from moment to moment. The sensible world is a world of constant change, of coming into existence and passing away. How can one obtain certain knowledge of anything if, during the process of studying it, it is becoming something else? In other words, Plato associated reality with an eternal changing truth. The real world, for him, consisted of a world of eternal ideas, existing in their own right independently of any mind and beyond the every-day world of sense-perceptions. They were not conceived by Plato as ideas in the sense we would use the term today but rather as patterns or forms of which the objects in the every-day world are imperfect copies. In one form or another this Platonic denial of the reality of the sense-perceived world continues to haunt philosophy. Whitehead truly said that Western philosophy since Plato is nothing but a series of foot-notes to his writings.

The form of this denial against which Marxists have launched their strongest criticisms derives from the theories of Locke, Berkeley and Hume. The latter's writings, in par-ticular, still strongly influence much contemporary philo-sophy. Indeed, he is described by one modern philosopher as 'Our Eldest Contemporary'.[7] It may prove useful to outline their views both to show in what relation they stand to Marxism and the kind of interpretation one may make of them in the light of Freudian theory.

John Locke challenged the view that the mind possessed knowledge that did not depend upon prior experience; knowledge, that is to say, that was *a priori* in character. His philosophy came to be known as *Empiricism* because of its stress upon the part played by experience in the acquisition of knowledge in contrast to the rationalist philosophies of Descartes, Spinoza and Leibniz. They were called rationalists, not in the sense that we use the term today, but because they believed that the possession of *a priori* knowledge enabled the mind by reasoning alone to arrive at truths. Locke's view-point may be summed up in his phrase: 'There is nothing in the understanding which was not first in the senses.' In other

<hr>

[7] Third Programme Talk, 13.5.62. Stuart Hampshire.

words, experience first, then knowledge and understanding.

Locke believed that the qualities which an object appears to have are of two kinds – those that belong to the object itself and those that exist only as ideas in the observer's mind. To the first qualities he gave the name primary qualities, and to the second, secondary qualities.

Primary qualities, in Locke's view, are the qualities of size, position, weight, shape; i.e. the qualities connected with the extension of the object in space. They were considered by Locke to belong to the object in its own right because under all circumstances the object displayed them. An object always has shape, position, size, but its colour, temperature and smell vary according to circumstances. Thus in the dark an object has no colour; its smell and taste will depend upon conditions in the observer; if, for example, he has a bad cold it will appear to him to have no taste or smell. Hence these latter qualities cannot be said, Locke argued, to belong to the object itself. They were secondary qualities existing as ideas in the observer's mind, produced by the effect of the object on his senses and referred by him back to the object.

Further, Locke believed in the existence of a 'substance' in which the primary qualities were supposed to inhere. Although he acknowledged that we have no experience of such a substance, it was considered by Locke to be a necessary postulate by which the various qualities of an object could be related together. It provided a support, or substratum, for them.

Such was the viewpoint of Locke in opposition to which Berkeley developed his philosophy. Berkeley agreed that secondary qualities existed only as ideas in our minds,[8] but he claimed that this is true of primary qualities also. The distinction between primary and secondary qualities, he argued, was invalid. For we acquire our knowledge of the shape and position of objects in exactly the same way as we do our knowledge of their taste, colour and smell, namely, through our sense-perceptions. Both primary and secondary

[8] Or in God's mind, as we shall see later.

qualities are ultimately sense-perceptions. To argue beyond these sense-perceptions to some 'substance' in which they are supposed to inhere is to go beyond the immediacy of our sense-perceptions. It is to violate the principle of empiricism enunciated by Locke, that there is nothing in our understanding that is not first in our senses. We have no sense-experience of a 'substance' and therefore have no right to postulate its existence.

For Berkeley, then, the whole of external reality, not just part of it, exists as ideas in our minds. To exist, said Berkeley, is to be perceived ... 'all the choir of heaven and furniture of earth have not any subsistence without a mind in that their being is to be perceived or known'.

What, then, happens to objects when they are no longer being perceived by us? Do they then cease to exist? Berkeley replied that all objects are perceptions in God's mind. It is, indeed, from the Eternal Mind of God, he said, that our ideas flow. Hence, when we cease to perceive them, they nevertheless continue to exist by reason of Divine Perception.

But Berkeley, by this answer, had in his turn exposed himself to the charge of inconsistency. The charge was made by the Scottish philosopher, David Hume.

Hume accepted Berkeley's view that reality was compounded of sense-perceptions. But he pointed out that we have no direct sense experience of God. And as, according to Berkeley himself, we have no grounds for believing in anything that is not directly given in sense perceptions, we have no right to invoke the existence of God. Thus the argument that Berkeley had used against Locke to the effect that we have no direct sense-experience of a 'substance' was directed against himself. For Locke's substance, Berkeley had substituted God. Both viewpoints transcend the knowledge given in our sense-perceptions and therefore both viewpoints are equally invalid.

Hume did not rest with his criticism of Divine Perception. He turned his logical mind to ordinary, human perception, to the notion of a self that perceives. Again he appealed to direct experience. There is nothing in direct experience to justify the idea of a self, he claimed. Thus: 'when I enter most intimately into what I call myself, I always stumble on some particular perception or other, of heat and cold, light or shade, love or hatred, pain or pleasure. I never can catch myself at any time without a perception.' Mankind he continues, 'is nothing but a bundle or collection of different perceptions, which succeed each other with an inconceivable rapidity and are in a perpetual flux and movement.'

From these criticisms of Hume, Marxists have been quick to point out there follows an important logical conclusion, a conclusion that no consistent idealist can avoid. For if external reality has only existence as ideas or perceptions in our minds and if the only ideas of which we can have immediate knowledge are our own, then we must conclude that external reality is our idea. Or rather 'my' idea; for each of us can only speak of his own ideas. The 'my' is a courtesy pronoun only, for the idealist strictly has no logical right to postulate even his own existence. His knowledge of himself is presumably based upon sense-impressions and, in terms of his own theory, cannot be considered to be indicative of a reality beyond them. If he claims that he has knowledge of his own reality transcending his own sense-impressions then he is abandoning the mainplank of idealist theory, namely, that we can have no knowledge transcending that given in our sense-perceptions. In other words the idealist is not just forced into a solipsist position in which he asserts that only he exists and the rest of the world are ideas of his mind; he is not allowed to assume his own existence. He cannot know, on his own showing, that he, himself, exists. But in order to formulate his solipsist position he must assume his own existence as something to which sense-perceptions are occurring. And in doing so he involves idealism in self-contradiction.

The philosophy of Immanuel Kant, in one sense, is an attempt to overcome the solipsist difficulty of idealism. It does so by postulating a world outside human thought, a world, however, whose real nature is unknowable. Thus, Kant distinguished between the world as it appears to us in our sense-perceptions and the world as it is in itself. The world of our sense-perceptions he termed the phenomenal world; the world beyond our sense-perceptions, or the world in itself, he termed the noumenal world. Between these two worlds, he argued, is an unbridgeable gulf. For our minds are so constituted that they impose certain general qualities upon whatever we perceive. Thus, we perceive objects in space and time and related as cause and effect, not because they really exist in space and time and are related as cause and effect but because the nature of the mind is such that it gives these qualities to whatever is perceived.

Kant based this view upon the postulate that the mind possesses a priori knowledge which it combines with the knowledge gained through sense-experience. His arguments for the existence of a priori knowledge run somewhat as follows:

Children have no accurate knowledge of distances or perspectives yet are able to discern what objects are in front of them, which behind and which beside them. They reach out for those that please them and turn from those that do not. This knowledge of spatial relations, of before, behind, besides, requires no prior experience. Children just have it. Hence, argued Kant, the idea of space is an a priori idea. It exists prior to any kind of experience. If the child did not begin with this idea of space, his sense-perceptions would be a chaotic muddle. But by means of his pre-existing idea of space he is able to order and to relate together his experiences. His idea of space combines with his experience of things in such a way that he perceives things as existing in space. Similarly with time. The child appears to have ideas of before and after, now and then, which do not depend upon prior experiences. He thus imposes a temporal order upon events in the same way as he imposes a spatial order.

From mathematics Kant derived his strongest argument for the existence of a priori knowledge. A proposition such as two plus two equal four, or the three angles of a triangle are equal to two right angles, is true in all circumstances. We have a conviction of their truth which is independent of our experience. For we can only experience a limited number of cases in which these propositions may be shown to be true. And if experience were the deciding factor, we should only be entitled to pronounce upon these few cases. Yet we unhesitatingly believe that these propositions are true in all cases. We state them as self-evident truths. This, said Kant, is because we intuitively know them to be true in all cases. We have a priori knowledge to that effect. And as mathematics refers chiefly to space and time relations, it establishes the a priori nature of space and time.

The stress that Kantian philosophy lays on the gulf between the world as it appears to us and the world as it is in itself, seems to gain some strength from modern physics. For modern physics gives evidence of the complex process by which sense-perceptions of external objects arise in our minds. Stimuli from an object in the form of light waves, for example, impinge on the nerve-endings in the eye and cause a complex series of electrical and chemical changes to take place there. These are propagated along the optic nerve to the brain where a disturbance takes place in the visual cortex and we declare that we see the object. Between the object in the outer world and these disturbances in the visual cortex that constitute our perception of it there are, thus, several stages of transformation, which make it extremely improbable, it is argued, that the end product of this complicated neural process resembles even remotely the object in the outer world which begun it. The most that can be said about it, is that it stands in some symbolic relation to the object and that by clever manipulation of the symbol it is possible to influence the object symbolised. So runs the argument from modern physics.

Against these arguments which still exert a powerful influence, Marxism opposes a robust, commonsensical realism. The Marxist technique as we have seen is to classify as

idealist any view that makes the existence of the external
world dependent partly or wholly on mental processes, and
then to show that such a view inescapably reduces to
solipsism. It asserts that we test the accuracy of our knowledge
of the external world in practice, that the extent of our control over the external world proclaims the accuracy of our
notions concerning it.

This is a view that was shared by Freud. 'If there were no
knowledge,' he wrote, 'which was distinguished from among
our opinions by the fact that it corresponds with reality, then
we might just as well build our bridges of cardboard as of
stone, or inject a tenth of a gramme of morphia into a patient
instead of a hundredth, or take tear gas as a narcotic instead
of ether.'[9]

Marxists tend not to spend much time examining the
subtleties of the idealist arguments. Instead, they steamroller
over them with their insistence upon the solipsist implication
of all forms of idealism. In place of it, they offer a copy or
reflection theory of the relation of knowledge to the external
world which seems in conflict with the more dynamic aspects
of their thinking. Lenin, and to some extent, Engels, made
much of the notion that our ideas reflect the external world
somewhat in the way that a mirror reflects objects. Thus
Lenin wrote: 'Matter is a philosophic category which refers
to the objective reality given to man in his sensations – a
reality which is copied, photographed, and reflected by our
sensations, but which exists independently of them.'[10]

This is a notion, I think, that derives from the tendency to
regard perception as primarily a function of vision.

When we ask – does the world in itself really 'look' as it
appears to us, we are, unconsciously, using the analogy of the
relation between a photograph and the object photographed
or a mirror and the object mirrored. But we do not usually
ask whether objects really smell and sound, in themselves, as

[9] *New Introductory Lectures* (Hogarth Press), p. 226.
[10] V. I. Lenin, *Materialism and Empirio-Criticism* (Martin Lawrence,
1927), pp. 101-2.

they smell and sound to us. We do not use the analogy for senses other than sight.

It seems to me more useful to think of our perceptions not so much as reflections of the world but as reactions or responses to it. When we say that we are seeing the world, we are responding visually to it. If we think of it in this way, the question whether the world is as we see it; whether our ideas correctly mirror or reflect it, need not arise in this misleading form.

To see our relation to the world as a responsive one is not to deny the reality of the external world. We are, after all, in the world, a part of it, not apart from it. Our history as mankind is part of the history of the world. This much Marxism has consistently stressed. But the nature of our relationships with other parts of the world is far more complex than it has allowed. In its whole-hearted rejection of idealism it forgets its own insistence upon the active nature of man's thinking, its criticisms of mechanical materialism which sees man as the passive sport of environmental pressures. Idealist philosophers have understood the active character of mental life but have been unable to relate it to the world of social reality. They have thought about it abstractedly, in separation from the world, a process that has required the development of a science of psychology for its correction.

This is the point that Marx himself seemed to be making when he wrote: 'Thus it happened that the *active* side, in opposition to materialism, was developed by idealism – but only abstractly. . . .'

The hint contained in these words has hardly been noticed by Marxists. It is a hint as to the direction in which materialism should be developed. Materialism, using scientific methods, must conquer the realms of subjective life, hitherto left to the abstract mystifications of idealist philosophers. To reject the methods of idealism, in-so-far as they depend upon intuitional and speculative considerations isolated from social reality, is one thing. But to deny the existence of the mental activity about which idealism speculates is quite another matter. It is a philosophical emptying of the baby with the bathwater.

Contemporary interest in psychology and in psycho-analysis in particular, is an important reflection of the type of problem that now faces mankind. Man, Marx has observed, occupies himself with those problems whose solution are within reach and bound up with his further progress. Hitherto science has been too busy conquering the world of external nature to give much time to the problems posed by man's inner nature. But now these problems claim priority in consideration. They demand to be taken from the realm of philosophical speculation and subjected to the rigorous discipline of science. Russell made the point that philosophical questions are those with which science is not yet ready to deal. Science is now ready to deal with the nature of those mental processes which do more than merely reflect the world in perceptions, ideas and concepts. It seeks to learn how man's wishes, hopes, fears, doubts, actively influence his picture of reality. Social reality is something interposed by man between himself and the natural, geographical environment. This much Marxists assert. But this social reality is shot through and through with irrationalities, with practices and ways of thought that betoken man's continuing emotional immaturity. Psycho-analysis is the first, important step in understanding the source and nature of this immaturity. No philosophy, no world outlook, that wants to be more than an academic exercise in speculation can afford to ignore the contribution of Freudian theory, can afford, indeed, not to make it an integral part of itself. This goes for Marxism in particular. For it is the most serious contemporary attempt to build a world outlook in which man's relation to the universe is a basic feature.

9

Some Applications

My aim in the preceding chapters has been to show that psycho-analysis and Marxism are complementary, mutually enriching approaches to the study of man. This has required that I outline both approaches in some detail, leaving on one side many related problems in order not to disturb the general pattern of my exposition. In this final chapter I propose to consider some of these problems, using it, as it were, as a clearing house.

But first I wish to stress that the Freudian-Marxist approach is not a substitute for detailed research; it supplies no ready-made answers to our problems. What it does is to provide a perspective, an orientation, a general framework, for considering problems and suggesting lines of research. Thus, if, in the light of this approach, we turn to the major conflicts of our day, we shall look, not only for the objective social and political factors that underly these conflicts but also for the personal subjective factors that tend to deepen and embitter them, increasing the obstacles to rational discussion. For example, the immediate causes of East-West tensions obviously arise because of the conflict of different economic, national and political aims embodied in different social systems. But they are intensified by suspicions, misunderstandings and anxieties that point to less rational causes and these require understanding if peaceful co-existence and, in consequence, human life is to be preserved on this planet. If there were regular international conferences of leading workers in the field of psychology to investigate the underlying irrational factors that bar the way to understanding, the tasks of statesmen meeting to discuss the problems that threaten world peace might well be made lighter.

Both Marxism and psycho-analysis, in their different ways, are studies of the irrational in man's life. Marxism studies the irrationalities of the social order that prevent men utilising to the full the technical discoveries that science has given them. Psycho-analysis studies the irrational forces in men's minds that thwart their development into mature, rational beings able to use science for their well-being. An irrational world situation demands a scientific study of irrationalities, whether subjectively or objectively considered. This is the justification for both the Freudian and Marxist approach.

It may be agreed that the present world situation does demand an intensive enquiry into the causal factors of these irrationalities but it may be asked: Do psycho-analysis and Marxism really qualify as scientifically valid forms of pursuing this enquiry? A scientific theory, it is often claimed, must have predictive capacity; it must enable us to look ahead, to forecast with reasonable accuracy, the trend of events.

We can see the main weight of this criticism, in particular, in regard to Marxism. Marxism is presented by its adherents as a scientific theory in which economic, historical and philosophical strands are woven into a world view. This world view, it is claimed, constitutes a guide to reality, particularly social reality.

The critics, however, contend that the chief prediction of Marx concerning the growth of society has been falsified by events. This was the prediction that the growth of capitalism would be accompanied by an increased misery of the masses. And this has not happened. Hence, Marxism is refuted.

The irrelevance of this kind of criticism becomes clear when we consider what a scientific theory is designed to do. Its task is twofold, namely, to explain and to predict. On the explanatory level it takes a number of otherwise unrelated factors and makes sense of them, suggests generalisations which bring them together into a meaningful pattern. On the predictive level it seeks to direct our attention, in the light of this meaningful pattern, to what may be expected to happen in the future. In a sense, it seeks to expand its explanatory theory to cover factors not yet observed. But, and this is important because it is here that the critics of Marxism go wrong, the relation between a prediction and a theory on which it is based, is not a logically necessary one. The most a scientific theory can do is to suggest possible developments which may or may not take place without necessarily invalidating or confirming the theory. Some scientific theories have high predictive value, particularly in the physical sciences; others, particularly those of an anthropological nature, have a low predictive value. For the latter, the number of variables is too high to allow for a high degree of accuracy in prediction. A low predictive value is the rule rather than the exception for scientific theories in the general anthropological field. Their claims to be scientific rest more upon their explanatory value than their predictive value.

One might even say that their value is more important in their *post*-dictive scope, that is to say, their capacity to knit together, meaningfully, the present state of affairs with the past. This may be derided as a form of being wise after the event, but is this really to be despised? This is, after all, what is meant by learning from experience, deriving wisdom after events so that we may come to anticipate them. At present, our anticipations, in the field of anthropological research, are uncertain and can only be stated in very general form. When, for example, Marx forecast the increasing misery of the masses as capitalism developed, he was far too specific, and people have seized upon this and claimed that events have

refuted him. But if, instead, he had forecast a growing instability of capitalism, a growing sense of insecurity and
irrationality, would he have seemed so far wrong? A strong
case can be made out for saying that, in principle, his prediction has been fulfilled even though its detailed form has
turned out somewhat differently.[1]

Criticisms of Freudian theory, as of Marxism, are generally
based on narrow views of the function of science, a confusion
concerning the role of theory in science. In one sense, the
term theory may be used in science very much in the way it is
used in detective stories. There is a missing link in a chain of
evidence that the detective seeks to bridge with a theory.
With further investigations the theory becomes a fact, the
missing piece of evidence is unearthed. In the same way, the
circulation of the blood or the source of the River Nile were
theories until the relevant facts were discovered.

In this sense, theory refers to an absent fact, a point made
by the American Behaviourist, Professor B. F. Skinner.
Science, in other words, may be regarded as an attempt to
describe and classify the phenomena of nature.

[1] The advent of automation has extended man's control and relative
independence of nature to an extent that Marx could not have foretold. But
this control remains within the confines of an economy geared to production
for profit. Hence its blessings, in the form of increased leisure, have not
passed, to any great extent, to the majority of people for whom automation
still carries the threat of unemployment. (Or redundancy, as the new term
is, a term which has passed into popular currency, taking odd shapes in
the process. One woman told me recently that her husband had been
'redunded'.) Nevertheless, some of this leisure, often through the pressure
of trades union activity, has spread throughout society, a process in which
labour-saving devices has helped. This increase in leisure poses serious
psychological problems which seem unlikely to be solved within the framework of our present society. It is true that there has been an increase in
do-it-yourself activities, home decoration, gardening and so forth. And this
is to the good. But the economic insecurity that still exists for many people
and which often touches off emotional insecurity derived from family relationships, leads many to use their leisure in pursuit of the fantasies engen-
dered by their insecurities. The increase in gambling, both on horses and
football pools, speaks eloquently of this. In addition, entertainments with
violence and sex as dominant themes canalise their frustrations. The reconstruction of society for which Marxists press, requires more than the removal
of economic barriers. We need to know much more about the psychological
needs which find expression in leisure pursuits, if cultural life is to match
the opportunities afforded by increased leisure.

But there is another sense, in which science plays a unifying role; in which hypotheses are suggested by which otherwise disparate facts are brought together and their interrelations economically and meaningfully exhibited. Such hypotheses may be valuable in suggesting further spheres of enquiry, or predicting the future course of events. But while prediction in human affairs is bound to be limited, it does not follow that we should only busy ourselves with those aspects of human activity that lend themselves to quantitative and statistical expression, a view that those critics of Freud who complain of his amateurism and lack of science, seem to suggest.

The scientific approach is the approach of people, ready to observe patiently and carefully, framing their theories without reference to their own personal likes or dislikes, testing their theories in practice where possible and abandoning them when new facts tell against them.

If the scientist is dealing with subject matter that can be measured and expressed quantitatively, he will measure. But if the subject-matter is not measurable, he will not therefore abandon it. He will be content with broad, explanatory generalisations, seeking to express as economically as possible the relationships among otherwise disconnected facts. This is what Freud has sought to do. In the words of a modern critic of Freud, who is fair enough to recognise Freud's achievements: 'The Freudian revolution consisted in *firstly*, establishing the fact that neuroticism, sexual perversions, and the aberrations of "normal" people represent immaturities of one kind or another, and *secondly*, introducing the concepts of causality and determinism in these fields. The description of the various ego-defence mechanisms by which we shelter from a hostile reality and from internal reproaches and criticism is based on acute empirical observation. These are Freud's permanent contributions to human knowledge.'[2]

An example to show both the limitations of the Anti-

[2] John McLeish—*The Science of Behaviour* (Barrie and Rockliff with Pemberton Publishing Co.), 1963, p. 157.

Freudian approach and the importance of Freudian explanatory concepts may be to the point here. In a chapter on
Psychological Theory in his book *The Dynamics of Anxiety
and Hysteria*[3] Professor Eysenck argues for what he calls an a-
historical approach. By this he appears to mean that when
confronted with a symptom which a Freudian would suggest
points to underlying causative factors, we should consider a
search for such factors to be superfluous. The symptom is
simply a bad habit that has somehow been acquired, and
which must be unlearned. 'Symptoms are learned S-R (stimu-
lous-response) connections, i.e. once they are extinguished or
deconditioned treatment is complete. Such treatment is based
exclusively on present factors.' He draws his main evidence
from the treatment of enuresis (bed-wetting) by a conditioning procedure. Enuresis, in children, is generally accompanied by anxiety and lack of self-confidence and it is true, as
my own experience in a Child Guidance Clinic confirms, that
clearing up this condition often leads to a reduction in
anxiety and increased self-confidence. Some form of bell-
alarm apparatus is used, generally consisting of two meshes of
wire which are separated by one bed-sheet, and covered by
another. The meshes are connected to a battery. When the
child voids urine it penetrates the top sheet and eventually
seeps through to the mattress, causing a short-circuit between
the meshes. This rings an alarm, and awakens the child who
is then expected to get out of bed, switch off the alarm and
complete the voiding of urine in the lavatory. In time the
child wakes with a full bladder without voiding urine, and
therefore before the bell rings. The waking response, which
at first was elicited by the bell, is now elicited by the fullness
of the bladder; it has, i.e. become conditioned to it. And, in
many cases, this does have a generally beneficial psychological
effect on the child but it is not clear that all that is involved is
the setting up of a conditioned response. For this treatment is
accompanied by interest and concern by adults in a psychiatric team, who maintain a non-critical and sympathetic atti-

[3] Page 268. Routledge and Kegan Paul (1957).

tude throughout. This was made clear to me in a rather curious way. I found that a number of parents of children who had been supplied with these apparatuses, had not understood how to use them either through inadequate instruction or sheer forgetfulness. In any case, the alarms did not go off but nevertheless the children's bedwetting cleared up. There is also evidence of success in remedying this condition through hypnosis and simple suggestion. Thus some psychiatrists give the child a record sheet on which to note the days and nights when he is dry and this also seems to have a therapeutic effect. What I think is happening in these cases is that the encouragement and sympathetic interest of psychiatrists, psychologists and social workers, support and strengthen the child's ego so that he can more effectively face his problem. An explanation in terms of conditioning theory is far too limited; it requires the more comprehensive approach of Freudian theory to make sense of what has happened.

But there is still another reason why the historical approach of Freud is important and why, indeed, the a-historical refusal to look beyond the presenting symptoms may be harmful. For this refusal deflects attention from psychological and social conditions that may be responsible for producing much unhappiness. On the social level, we know, from the work of Burt and Stott, that slum conditions and broken homes are important contributory factors in maladjustment in childhood while the more subtle psychological relationships within the family, the loves and hates which may be generated make their contribution also.[4] Not to look beyond the presenting symptoms may not only be hard on a particular child needing help but holds up research into the predisposing conditions for maladjustment in general. After all, it is still true that prevention is better than cure.

To sum up. It seems that certain critics of Freud and Marx

---

[4] *Delinquency and Human Nature*, D. H. Stott (Carnegie United Kingdom Trust) 1950.
    The Young Delinquent, Cyril Burt (University of London Press) 1944.

tend to have too narrow a view of what science involves. Freud and Marx belong to those geniuses of human history who provide comprehensive, unifying theories richly suggestive of further lines of inquiry. Science expresses man's efforts to understand both external nature and himself. In some fields his knowledge may give him control but it is not only for the purpose of control that man wants to know. This is the error of the narrow empiricism of those who criticise the work of Freud and Marx. We want to understand, whether it brings control or not, because this answers an important human need.

At the beginning of this chapter I stressed that Freudian and Marxist theory provide a broad perspective from which to view problems of contemporary life rather than supplying detailed answers to these problems. I propose now, in conclusion, to illustrate this approach by looking at some major social and political problems that are closely interrelated.

We shall begin with the world of politics. Politics is the art of government, the ordering of economic and social life of a community. It calls for the exercise of power, for the institution of rules and practices by which men's social relationships may be regulated so that social life may proceed with a minimum of conflict.

The main contribution of Marxist theory to political theory has been to stress that politics, in class-differentiated societies, tends to seek the perpetuation of the power of one or more ruling classes. Harmony among the classes, it suggests, is achieved by a joint process of presenting, through educational and propaganda media, the interests of the ruling classes as if they were the interests of the whole community and of repressing opposition to their rule, when it achieves dangerous proportions. What is interesting about the Marxist concept of politics is that it includes a notion of the State as something much more extensive than the governmental or parliamentary machinery for making laws. By the State, is meant all the means of directing social life – the judiciary, the armed forces, the schools, the police, the press – through which the will of dominating classes may be imposed, directly or indirectly, upon the rest of society. This view of the state has been criticised as being at once too narrow and too general, too narrow because it identifies government policy with sectional interests and too general because it includes, in the ruling power, relatively independent bodies such as the press and judiciary. This criticism seemed more valid when the growth of parliamentary democracy held a prospect, for young and vigorous political parties, of a relatively smooth transformation of society through the acquisition of a majority of parliamentary seats. The criticism has lost much point today with a growing awareness that power to rule and determine the course of national events does not reside exclusively in government hands. The Marxist theory of the state has re-appeared in the notion of the Establishment, a somewhat vague and confused notion at present but one that is quickly taking coherent shape. It represents a growing recognition that a progressive-minded government, bent on radical social changes, has more to meet than an opposition in parliament. The Marxist view at least has called attention to the complex character of political reality. It cannot be reduced to a simple majority-minority relationship of political parties.

In one sense, the Marxist theory of the State asserts that obedience to the State depends more upon the habits, traditions, the psychological acceptance of a ruling class, than upon the use of physical powers of coercion.

In other words, the State ordinarily depends upon creating a submissive attitude in the mass of people, on persuading them to accept its authority. A State that depended solely or almost solely upon repression and coercion would quickly cease to exist. Its strength lies in the hold it has on the minds of people. And this raises the important question as to the nature of the psychological factors that give the State its power over people's minds.

Political theorists, with little interest in the psychological aspects of politics, supply an answer to this question in terms of utilitarian or rational motives. Professor Laski, for example, suggested that men obey the State because a rational calculation shows them that, on balance, they get more out of obeying it than disobeying it. 'They scrutinise those orders (of the State) in terms of the satisfactions they seek from life, and from time to time they reject them upon the ground that they are a denial of those satisfactions.'[5] Unfortunately, obedience to the State rarely takes such rational form. In a sense it is true that people obey for the satisfactions they get out of this obedience but these satisfactions are not entirely of the kind subject to rational calculation. In fact, people often obey the State long after it has proved incapable of giving them the kind of satisfactions that rational calculation would demand. People will endure poverty, bad housing, lack of food with little sign of revolt. Their habits of obedience have deep, irrational roots. The satisfactions they seek are not primarily those that can be expressed in terms of living conditions.

It is here that Freudian theory takes over. The Marxist premiss that the power of the State depends upon many invisible bonds of tradition and habit as well as upon coercion, is given psychological content in Freudian theory. For the State derives its psychological power largely from its superego role. It provides an external support for the need for guidance and authority that we retain from childhood days.

The State, in other words, draws a psychological strength from the authority of the father as he appears to the child's mind. This explains the irrational features of loyalty and obedience to a State even when it neglects the elementary economic needs of its people. So long as the State presents a strong and confident front, people will tend to obey it with little question. They will be responding much as a child does to the authority of a powerful father. But let weaknesses

[5] *The State in Theory and Practice* (Allen & Unwin, 1935), p. 17.

appear in the ruling class; let it become torn by indecision and conflict; let defeat in war expose the population to famine or destruction, and the psychological power of the State is severely shaken. It is no accident that defeat in war has provided the impetus for many revolutions. Lenin defined the conditions for the success of a revolution, placing prominently among them the dissipation of confidence by the people in the ruling class. The Freudian theory makes sense of the uncritical aspects of the acceptance of State rule. And it also makes sense of the fierceness with which revolt against the State is fought. For it is the unleashing of repressed hostility, the hatred that children often unconsciously feel for their parents, leading them at times to outbursts of temper and fits of destruction.

That political life affords enormous scope for power-seeking individuals who derive from the hurly-burly of political life a strong sense of self-importance carries many dangers. For it means that people who seek to enter politics from a sense of devotion to their fellows, a desire to right social wrongs, will tend to be thrust aside by the more vigorous, clamorous and ruthless aspirants to political power. This was the problem that faced Plato in the construction of his Republic; how to get people, rational and genuinely devoted to the public good, to assume political leadership? He knew, and it remains true today, that such qualities of character go along with modesty and distaste for the cut and thrust of political struggle. Politics is regarded as a dirty business and we hand the conduct of our affairs to people who revel in the intrigues and deceptions of the political world. As science places greater powers in our hands, the danger from these people correspondingly grows. The fate of the world balances precariously on interpretations of 'national honour' by small groups of politicians. Politicians, whose major qualification for ruling is that they have more powerful personalities, more drive and ambition, than most other people, are able to take decisions involving the life and security of their fellows.

The process by which power has become concentrated in fewer hands in modern states so that one man may make vital decisions without even consulting his cabinet, is graphically described by Professor Geoffrey Barraclough. Members of parliament, he writes, have been transformed into voting machines. 'They cannot vote against their party; they cannot even abstain; they have no right to independent judgement on questions of substance, and they know that if they fail to follow the party line they can have no expectation of re-election. The one indispensable quality demanded of them, in short, is party loyalty, and the theory of classical representative democracy, that the electors should choose a candidate for his ability and personality, has ceased to count....'[6] As loyalty to party means ultimately loyalty to party leader, we have a situation today which conforms remarkably well with the Freudian analysis of political relationships.

We clearly need more research into the motives that lead some people into politics, particularly those for whom the goal of power over the lives of others has a magnetic appeal. Politics is not something which everyone, or even most people actively engage in. People who join political parties, and especially those who play an active part in them, form quite a small minority of the public. For most people, politics is something they read about, or indulge in every now and again at elections and at times of major crisis. To be political all the year round is to be quite a peculiar person. The problem for the psychologist is not only that of discovering why some people are drawn to political activity but also why it takes the form it does, why some tend towards conservatism and others towards radicalism. I use these terms in their literal rather than their political sense. Thus within the political party of the Conservatives, or the Labour or the Communists, one finds people who are more cautious than others; some more adventurous and so on. This pattern roughly of left, centre and right, figures in all parties.

[6] G. Barraclough, *An Introduction to Contemporary History* (Watts) 1964.

Marxism can tell us why people join the Conservative, Labour, Liberal or Communist parties in terms of economic interests. And, broadly speaking, we can detect a correlation between a person's economic status and his choice of political party. But there is still the puzzle as to why he shows leftist, centrist or rightist tendencies.

Some interesting research work has been done on this problem. Professor Eysenck, e.g., in his study *The Psychology of Politics*[7] argues for a Radical-Conservative dimension in personality structure. He used a questionnaire technique to find out what ideas go together among different supporters of the main political parties. He found clusters of ideas which showed that radicals tended to believe in easier divorce laws, gentler treatment of criminals, more freedom in education and so forth, while conservatives tended to believe in flogging as a deterrent against crime, the inferiority of coloured people, war as a natural activity and so on. While these ideas tended to be more marked in one political party than another, there was some spread among all political parties.

Other researches[8] suggest that people who play an active and forceful part in politics tend to have had more unhappiness in childhood, more feelings of rejection by their parents than those who remain relatively inactive. They tend to develop what Freudians call super-ego revolt, finding in political life scope for their repressed hostility.

What can be done about this? I can find no easy answer. I only know that in these days of menace of nuclear destruction, we must find some other way of choosing our political leaders. What we do today, after all, is this. We tend to choose our political leaders from among those people who thrust themselves forward for our choice. We give power to those who love it. Plato saw the danger in this, but we have not yet. Ours is a society in which the least suitable often volunteer for, and are given, the most responsible jobs. One can only

[7] Eysenck, *The Psychology of Politics* (Routledge & Kegan Paul), 1954.
[8] e.g. by M. H. Krout and R. Stagner.

hope that the dangerous situations in which our political
leaders have, from time to time, placed us will eventually
stimulate the more mature and rational among us to overcome their distaste for politics and seek to play a more active
role in the life of the community.[9]

We still have to ask: why are politicians able to win support for their claims to leadership? One factor, we have seen,
is that they have so much more drive than their fellows; to
achieve power is so much more important to them. But they
would never achieve their domination over the minds of their
fellows; their propaganda efforts would fall on barren soil,
were it not for a certain form of uncritical thinking to which
their efforts are directed. Political arguments make use of
stereotypes, a form of thinking which requires the minimum
of criticality. The term stereotype was first used by Walter
Lippmann to name a rigid way of speaking of whole groups of
people, pinning a label on them which more often than not
gave a grotesque caricature of them. To speak of all Italians
as 'wops', e.g., is to append a label to them, to apply a stereotype to them, which has a derogatory connotation. Coloured
people are 'niggers' by this procedure. Jews are thought to
conform with a stereotyped caricature of a shylock. This kind
of thinking is heavily charged with prejudice, in which strong
emotionally-toned beliefs are held independently of factual
evidence. The prejudiced person, thinking in terms of
stereotypes, is generally impervious to any rational arguments. He clings to his beliefs obstinately; they fulfil a
psychological need for him. They are defensive responses to
fears and anxieties with infantile roots.

This has been confirmed by research into the psychological
sources of racial prejudice. While there may be economic

[9] This is not to say that we do not sometimes have leaders of wisdom
moved largely by a desire to serve the community. The late President
Kennedy, e.g., showed a maturity of judgement rarely equalled by other
occupants of positions of power. To desire power for oneself and to desire
to do good for others, are not necessarily exclusive characteristics. But they
can conflict at critical points, when, e.g. personal prestige is at stake. It is not
easy for a leading politician to admit an error of judgement, to risk losing
face, even though the lives of many people may be at stake.

factors involved, they tend to trigger off, rather than gener-
ate, the hostilities expressed in anti-negro and anti-semitic
attitudes. An extensive investigation carried out in California
U.S.A. showed that men and women strongly prejudiced
against minorities, tended to have had dominating parents
who applied harsh discipline and demanded unquestioning
obedience. The research[10] used the method of attitude scales
in which subjects are asked to indicate the degree of their
agreement or disagreement with a number of statements.
Thus in a scale on anti-semitism one statement read: 'In
order to maintain a nice residential neighborhood it is best
to prevent Jews from living in it.' Subjects who scored high
in prejudice showed, on further analysis, considerable repressed hostility to their parents and a tendency to project
this hostility upon convenient targets. The convenient target
for unscrupulous politicians today is, of course, coloured
people.

The appeals to infantile forms of thinking and attempts to
harness fears and anxieties to political parties, have today become a deliberately planned procedure. Advertising agencies
and public relations organisations having learned from Freud
something of the substructure of the human psyche, are
exploiting this knowledge to gain support for their political
paymasters. A new technique has grown up of tapping
people's fears, hopes, anxieties and utilising them in the sale,
originally of goods, and now of political parties and personalities. This technique is known as motivational research
and has spread from the United States where its main directing force has been Dr. Ernest Dichter. Psychologists are employed to detect people's weaknesses, their anxieties and uncertainties, their unconscious wishes and hopes in order that
sales campaigns may be organised which allow for, and
capitalise on, these factors. Cleverly worked out interview
techniques enable the exploration by trained workers, often
psychologists, of mental processes lying outside the normal

[10] Reported in *The Authoritarian Personality* by T. W. Adorno, E. Frenkel-
Brunswik, D. J. Levinson, R. N. Sanford (New York: Harper, 1950).

range of consciousness. The individual is led to expose his private doubts and anxieties to the skilled researcher who can then suggest ways by which these doubts and fears may be manipulated in the interest of the product to be marketed.

In his book *The Strategy of Desire*[11] Dr. Dichter illustrates the skilful use of Freudian notions in his approach to the consumer. He writes: 'During one specific year, one of the new car models happened to have a very blunt bonnet, and this particular model turned out to be a complete flop. For a long time, the reason for this flop was attributed to purely technical reasons. Actually, what had happened was that this car manufacturer had run foul of one of the irrational factors at work in human nature. The normal shape of a car has a lot to do with its symbolic significance, that of a penetrating instrument. It symbolises speed and power; it has, further-more, in a psychological sense, considerable significance as a phallic symbol. In a sense, therefore, when the model with the blunt bonnet came onto the market, it violated this sym-bolic significance of the shape of the car, and it was rejected instinctively by people who did not know why. In other words, to them it lacked a certain sense of potency and penetrating power.' Dr. Dichter concludes: 'It is very impor-tant that the man whose job it is to persuade others should be aware of this peculiarity of human nature. If he is not, he is bound to make tremendous mistakes.'

The exploitation of people's hopes and fears, as a tech-nique employing the insights and discoveries of Freud, has moved into the field of politics. The voting public is treated as a market to be developed, in which goods are to be sold. The choice between political parties is being presented, as one newspaper put it, as a choice between rival detergents. What is becoming more and more important is not the policies of the parties but the emotional impact of party leaders. The universality of the television viewing habit has aided this process. Leading politicians are groomed for tele-

[11] Dichter: *The Strategy of Desire* (Boardman), 1961.

vision appearances; their policies presented with the slickness of a sales campaign.[12]

It might be argued that there is nothing essentially wrong in presenting one's policies in as attractive a manner as possible or grooming one's leaders for television appearances. This is a form of communication, of associating one's party with deep emotional needs and if one's policies are right, it cannot be harmful if they receive both the intellectual and emotional assent of the public.

The danger, of course, is that a temptation is always present to make the requirements of publicity prevail over the selection of leaders and political objectives. Thus if Mr. B has a better television personality than Mr. A this weighs in his favour in the selection of leaders. And if a particular aspect of one's policy presents publicity difficulties, it may be whittled down or even abandoned.

The remedy lies, to a large extent, in developing a more mature and critical public opinion, which would not lose sight of basic political issues. And this brings us to the problem of education.

Education tries to do two things. In the first place, it is a means of imparting knowledge to the young, giving them information over a wide range of subjects which, it is hoped, will be useful, either in a practical sense, or in the background sense of providing a cultural setting for later life. In the second place, education is supposed to stimulate in the child the ability to think critically and constructively, to learn how to work with others, to accept responsibility. In other words, to behave on the level of a mature, civilised

[12] An article in the *Observer* (20.1.63) showed an exceptionally keen insight into these new problems of leadership. Discussing the coming election of a new labour party leader following the death of Mr. Gaitskell, it said: 'Mr. Wilson's defeat in the contest for the deputy leadership does not of itself mean that he would be defeated in an election for the leadership itself. The party will now be looking for an experienced, acceptable public figure with a national reputation and the ability to compete on television against the Prime Minister and Mr. Grimond.

'Mr. Brown's victory last autumn does not necessarily mean that, in the eyes of the Parliamentary party, he fulfils these conditions. They are essential for a leader but not for his deputy.'

adult. It is with this second sense of education that I am concerned here, although the first sense is not entirely separate from it. Children who have been taught to think critically and accept responsibility are generally better able to master the more routine aspects of education.

Can we say that our educational system is succeeding in these tasks? If we take, as criteria, the kind of things people show interest in when they leave school; the kind of arguments that persuade them in politics, religion and other spheres of social life; the success of mass newspapers, mass advertising; the general level of television programmes, we must acknowledge that the level of critical and constructive thinking is very low indeed.

One important reason for this, I think, is that the physical conditions in which education takes place today make it very difficult to establish any other relationship than one of dominance by the teacher and submission by the children. Classrooms are so often badly equipped and overcrowded that free movement of the children is impossible. The teacher-child relationship, through force of circumstances, becomes patterned on the Victorian parent-child relationship in which the child speaks only when spoken to and the voice of the parent is supreme. It is true that many teachers do their best to overcome the limitations of class space and class size and strive to engage their children more actively in the lessons. But too often the criterion of a good class in present circumstances is a quiet class, where silence is broken only by the teacher's voice and the permitted responses to the teacher's questionings. Many teachers are little more than wardens controlling thirty or forty uncomfortably-seated lively animals.

These difficulties of the class situation are bound to influence the teacher's assessment of his pupils' behaviour. He will tend to see as a serious problem, behaviour expressing rebellion against his authority while behaviour which, from a psychological viewpoint, may seem more worthy of concern, may rate low in the teacher's scale of problems. This was shown in an interesting comparison of the ratings of teachers

and the staffs of Child Guidance Clinics in America. Five
hundred teachers composing the entire teaching staffs of
thirteen public elementary schools in New York, New Jersey,
Ohio and Minnesota were asked to rate the relative serious-
ness of fifty behaviour problems. Their ratings were compared
with those of thirty psychiatrists, psychologists and psychiatric
social workers. The report states: 'The most striking difference between the teachers' and the mental hygienists' ratings
is to be found in the comparative estimates of problems describing the withdrawing, recessive personality and behaviour traits. Whereas teachers considered shyness, sensitive-
ness, unsocialness, fearfulness, dreaminess among the least
serious of all problems, the mental hygienists ranked them
together with unhappiness, depression, easy discouragement,
resentfulness, cowardliness, suggestibility, and overcriticalness,
at the very top of the list as the most serious problems. . . . The
items describing defiance to authority – impertinence, impu-
dence, disobedience – which teachers considered very serious
appear near the bottom of the mental hygienists' list.'[13]

The reason for this contrast is that psychologically the
teacher takes over the rôle of parents but is often compelled
to play this rôle more sternly than he would wish. At home,
the child can generally move about more freely than in
school; he can speak more freely. At school his periods of
freedom are limited to the short time he is released from
lessons when he has a chance to discharge his pent-up activity.
Contrast children playing during a break in school with children playing during the holidays. In the first instance, they
tend to charge about, shouting and screaming, like animals
released from a close and uncomfortable confinement. In the
second, they are still lively and active but there is more control, more balance in their play. The school itself, in which
the child is supposed to learn how to fit himself for a free,
democratic way of life, tends to be modelled on a strict
autocracy, with a hierarchy extending downwards from the

[13] E. W. Wickman: *Teachers and Behaviour Problems* (The Common-
wealth Fund, New York, 1954).

headteacher, a situation which many teachers would wish to avoid but have thrust upon them through the shortcomings of school facilities.

The upshot of this, is to develop in the child an uncritical acceptance of authority, an acceptance of statements at their face-value, which he takes with him into the social world beyond the school. He is expected to accept, to conform, to obey with a minimum of criticism.

Freudian theory can tell us what psychological factors are involved in the production of this subservient, uncritical outlook. What guidance does it give for the development of mature, critical, self-reliant adults? What can our educational system learn from it?

Here, I think, it has to join forces with the general psychological inquiry into the learning process. Indeed, much of psycho-analytic thinking about the educational process is accepted, not only by psychologists, but most scientists interested in child development. One has only to refer to the discussions on child development held by the World Health Organisation Study Group in Geneva in 1956[14] to see how true this is. The keynote of the discussions was the need to recognise that children are not just small adults – an adult is not just an enlarged baby – but have needs of their own which have to be understood if their growth is to be healthy and complete. These needs are related to developmental levels and education must be designed to match these levels not only on the intellectual plane but on the emotional, also.

Psychologists who have studied the learning process, have argued that education is largely a matter of providing the child with a favourable environment in which the child's natural capacity to learn may flourish. The teacher, in other words, is part of the learning situation, stimulating the activity of learning. This attitude has led to research on problems concerning readiness to learn. Psychologists have pointed to a process of growth going on within the child that

---

[14] Published in 4 volumes as *Discussions on Child Development* (Tavistock Publications, 1960).

seems to require a minimum of external stimulation, a process known as maturation, and researches show that the capacity to learn depends very much on the level of maturation. This is clear in relation to the complex movements involved in walking. Many fond parents try to teach their children to walk at far too early an age. But whether early training in walking is given or not, children tend to walk about the same age, roughly 15 months. This is true, for example, of those social groups in which the mothers carry their babies around strapped to their backs, up to the age when a child can usually toddle. The child walks when there is the right degree of maturity of muscular growth and co-ordination. Indeed, to seek to encourage the child to walk before it is ready, may do it harm. And this, it is argued with considerable evidential support, is true of many other things. Thus to try to get a child to grasp certain aspects of arithmetic too soon may produce in the child an attitude towards the subject that never leaves him, an attitude of distaste and anxiety. The difficulties with which his early struggles with the subject meet, may stay with him throughout his life. Enlightened educationists are therefore suggesting that subjects be taught when they are within the maturation level of the child, a level that is not easy to decide and varies from child to child.

Modern forms of supplementing the activity of the teacher, as, for example, teaching machines, aim to arouse an active participation of the child in the learning process. Such machines are probably better described as *learning* machines, because they allow the child to control the pace of his learning and to correct his errors himself. In this way, the self-correcting quality parallels the natural process by which the child learns to perform many actions. When the child learns to walk, e.g., a constant process of adjustment and re-adjustment goes on, as the organism corrects the early miscalculations and stumblings.

This approach of education from the learning situation, seeking to improve it by stimulating active participation, is consistent with general Marxist theory. The Marxist would argue, of course, that education tends to be slanted in class societies so that the assumptions of these societies are un-critically accepted. But it would also argue that an improvement in education involves an improvement both in general social conditions and in learning techniques in the schools.

This, I think, is broadly true. But improved social conditions and learning techniques provide only a favourable environment in which the maturing intellectual and emotional life of the child may develop. Intellectually, we have seen, we need to be careful not to place the child in situations for which he is not yet ready. And this is true, too, of his emotional development. For just as a child who faces an intellectual problem for which he is not ready may develop a permanent difficulty in relation to it, so a child who faces an emotional problem too soon, may suffer lasting difficulty.

Freudian theory furnishes an excellent framework for such research. It points to developmental stages in emotional life much as Piagetian theory[15] does for intellectual life. From the Freudian standpoint, education is largely a problem of balancing the demands of the id against the demands of reality. It points to the need to reduce the anxiety resulting from a too severe super-ego, to strengthen the ego in its function of rational consideration. Translated into everyday terms, Freudian theory argues against too rigid discipline of the class-room, the over-restricting of children in their movements and speech. For these are the means by which the child's rational and critical qualities are hampered. This does not mean that Freudian theory requires complete free expression, the total lifting of all repression. It requires, how-

[15] Professor Jean Piaget of the University of Geneva has made a number of brilliant studies of the development of children's intellectual abilities (see, e.g. *The Language and Thought of the Child* (Routledge and Kegan Paul, 1949) and *The Child's Conception of the World* (Routledge and Kegan Paul, 1951). Broadly, he traces three main stages in this development. First is the sensori-motor stage up to the age of about two; in which there is a progressive growth of co-ordination of the child's reflexes in the manipulation of objects in the world; second, a stage from two to about eleven in which the child's thinking is very much tied to what is concretely present and is beginning to move to a level of more abstract, reflective thought. This last characterises the third stage.

ever, more scope for expression of emotional needs so that they can more effectively be canalised in socially acceptable ways.

The main form of discipline in schools today is largely the discipline imposed by the teacher. In primary schools this externally applied discipline presents few problems. The children are small; their teachers so much bigger, and refractory pupils in a class-room can be isolated and punished. As the children grow, discipline becomes more difficult to apply. Ideally, one would hope that as children grew older the need for discipline would diminish. But anyone who has taught children from eleven years onwards knows that this is not so. What has been missing in the early years is the opportunity to learn to work in an atmosphere of freedom. If children had early developed the habit of working with a minimum of restriction they would have acquired the habit of self-discipline and presented fewer disciplinary problems when older.

This is what Freudian theory would suggest, that the ego must be given scope to grow and strengthen itself; that the too early imposition of strict discipline discourages the growth of self-discipline. To make a virtue of obedience is to undermine self-dependence.

An important function of education is the development of value judgements in children and this is a process particularly dependent on the accepted standards and aims of a society. In fact, the values that children may be taught to regard as desirable, may conflict strongly with the values that predominate in society. Thus children may be taught that co-operation is good; that self-interest, as opposed to social welfare, is bad; that service to the community is better than self-enrichment, only to find in the wider social world a different, contradictory set of values in being. There is a stress on competition: on the pursuit of self-enrichment. Prestige and success are measured in terms of money. Even success in literature and art is measured in terms of money. The successful author or painter is the one making money. Money assumes a compulsive quality in men's lives. The millionaire drives on for another million. The Freudian symbolism for money is faeces and one cannot but feel that a description of capitalism as an anal-sadistic phase of social development is peculiarly apt.

The problem of education leads naturally to the problem of transition from childhood to adulthood – sometimes called the 'teenager' problem. Freudian and Marxist theory can give us, I think, an orientation in thinking about the problem, a readiness to notice economic and psychological factors that make important contributions to it.

The teenager is in the no man's land between childhood and adulthood. He (or she) is moving from a condition of dependence on adults – his parents and teachers in particular – to a condition in which he must take his place in society as an independent, self-reliant adult. Such a transition period has special problems in western civilisation although, of course, transition problems do not arise exclusively in our modern society. For any society, any cultural group, has to deal with the problem of the transition from childhood to adulthood. The fact that the child has to become a man or woman, taking a place in the life of the community, is common to all human groups. In our complex economic and social community, however, the business of becoming an adult has special features of its own that make the transition more difficult.

In a relatively simple society, boys and girls are expected to take their place in the community almost as soon as they are physically able to do so. When the boy is physically strong enough to take part in the hunting, fishing or agricultural life of the group and the girl is physically ready for child-bearing, they are inducted into the full life of the community through initiation ceremonies. The important point is that, in many cases, the introduction of the child to the responsibilities of adult life coincides fairly closely with the physical readiness of the child to take part in this life. When, i.e., the child is biologically ready for adult life he is automatically ready for it socially, also.

In our society, however, biological readiness for adult status is not considered sufficient qualification for the young person to take his place as an independent adult. For example, while a girl may be physically ready to bear children at the age of 13 and younger, our society considers that she is not ready for the social function of rearing a family until considerably later. Similarly, earning a living has become so complex a matter that many jobs require a level of education and training that takes young people well beyond their point of biological maturity. There is, thus, a gap between the biological readiness to perform adult functions and the social opportunities to do so, a gap that grows continuously. To put it briefly: underlying much of the teenager problem in our complex society is this simple fact: that teenagers are not considered to be ready socially to do the things that they are ready, biologically, to do.

Now this is a serious enough problem on its own. But it is exacerbated by the apparent ignorance of most adults of the nature of young people's problems. The adolescent is undergoing subtle physiological changes that arouse pressing demands. Glandular changes are taking place, speeding up his growth, filling out the body. Biologically, the body insistently demands what society denies it. In particular, society requires suppression of sex demands. It surrounds the subject of sex with a network of prohibitions and taboos. And the adolescent, who is becoming conscious of new bodily needs that he does not understand, and is expected to control, becomes uneasy and resentful about adult domination.

Bound up with these bodily changes are important psychological changes. The adolescent becomes more acutely aware of himself, more conscious of his, or her, body, more introspective. It is here that the conflict with adults intensifies. For parents often refuse to recognise that the growing adolescent has needs of his own. They continue to treat him as a dependent child and expect from him the subservience of a child. They seem to have little insight into the sensitivity that accompanies adolescent growth, the ease with which the youth's self-esteem can be wounded. The adolescent boy, or girl, suffering from feelings of thwarted self-expression indulges in self-pitying moods and vengeful fantasies. The adults seem to have forgotten their own youth.[16] The Freudians would say they have repressed its painful memories; are visiting upon the young the sins of their own fathers.

The teenagers turn to their own age-mates for security and acceptance. They form cliques and groups which replace family ties and give them a sense of belonging. These groups have their own rules concerning clothes, hair-styles and general behaviour. Sometimes these may seem absurd and pointless to adults but they play an important stabilising role in teenager life. They have a ritualistic element, serving to ward off the anxiety evoked by the emotional instability of adolescent growth. Their world, said a survey by *Life* of the rules among American youth, is one of many laws. 'They are capricious laws, changing or reversing themselves almost overnight. But while they are in effect, the laws are immutable and the punishment for violation is ostracism.'

The teenage problem is generally associated with the growth of delinquency. No one has satisfactorily defined delinquency. Broadly, one can say that it covers all forms of behaviour of young people not acceptable to those who lay down the rules of society. Rubin,[17] in his study of crime and delinquency, says tersely that delinquency is 'what the law says it is'. It covers such actions as persistent truancy, stealing, destructiveness, taking and driving away cars, obscene language, assaults. Figures for delinquency are difficult to assess as offences vary in kind and quantity but, in any case, they relate to a small minority only of young people.[18] Research

[16] The B.B.C. programme 'Juke Box Jury' sometimes strikingly shows this lack of insight into the needs of young people where a song may be derisively rejected by the adult members of the panel and enthusiastically acclaimed by the auxiliary panel of young listeners. One such occasion was when a song with the theme 'I may not live to see another day' brought scathing comments from the adult panel and acceptance by all members of the teenage panel. From the standpoint of an adult this, and many similar songs, sound maudlin and sentimental in a sickly way. But for young people, they touch off emotional trends reflecting their acute self-consciousness which easily turns to self-pity.

[17] S. Rubin, *Crime and Juvenile Delinquency* (Stevens 1961).

[18] Home Office statistics for indictable offences for 1962 give a figure of around 100,000 for young people up to the age of 20. The relative population is 14 million.

has concentrated mainly on social factors such as home conditions and the neighbourhood in which the delinquent lives. Attention has particularly centred on the effects of broken homes through death of a parent, divorce, separation, imprisonment and so on but the results of such researches are far from conclusive. Shaw and McKay compared delinquents and non-delinquents in respect of broken homes and found that approximately 43 per cent of the former and 36 per cent of the latter came from broken homes.[19] But they pointed out that the tensions and conflicts in the homes before the break may have been more disturbing for the child than the actual break. Stott's[20] researches show that the child may throw himself into a round of escapades to keep at bay the anxiety provoked by a conflictful home situation. He may even engage in delinquencies as an escape route from home, committing a crime and taking no precautions to avoid detection in a pathetic attempt to assure his removal from home.

Poverty also seems a contributory rather than a directly causal factor in producing delinquency. Harriett Wilson, in her study of delinquency and child neglect distinguishes neglect delinquency from other forms. A delinquent of this kind generally lives in a squalid home with parents who give him very little positive guidance and whose own relationships are extremely unstable. He may live in a district 'where lorry-skipping and shoplifting expeditions on a Saturday morning to Woolworth's are part of the game of living and he may join in this'.[21] His delinquencies are responses to an inadequate home, the early need to shift for himself teaching him to lay hold of anything within reach, no matter to whom it belongs.

But whatever the social factors, there seems to be an important psychological thread running through most cases of delinquency, namely a sense of not being wanted by parents, a feeling of rejection by them. Recent researches tend to centre attention on the father as the most important parent in this

[19] C. R. Shaw and H. D. McKay, *Social Factors in Juvenile Delinquency*—in Report on the Causes of Crime, Vol. II, U.S. Govt. Printing Office, 1931.
[20] D. H. Stott, *Delinquency and Human Nature*.
[21] Harriett Wilson, *Delinquency and Child Neglect* (Allen & Unwin 1962).

respect. Thus in his survey Psychology and Social Problems[22] Michael Argyle writes: 'Rejection is one of the major sources of delinquency. Rejection of a boy by his father is one of the best predictors of delinquency, 60 per cent of delinquents being so treated.'

It is here that research on psycho-analytic lines seems indicated. For most delinquents are boys[23] and their relationships to their fathers, following the pattern of the Oedipus situation, hold greater possibilities for mutual distrust and jealousy, with possible rejection by the father, than those of daughter and father.

However, the primary social problem of teenagers concerns the large number of young people who do not fall into delinquency but, none-the-less, find the culture in which they are growing up uninspiring, alien, and defeating.

It is sometimes argued that there is something special about the teenage problem today, something that is there even when we allow for the adult tendency to forget its own youthful follies. Whatever it is, it needs to be seen against the background of post-war insecurities and anxieties. For modern youth belongs to a generation that has barely emerged from the most destructive war in history, a time of upheaval and dislocation of which the youth of other generations had no similar experience. No one can assess the impact that these circumstances have had on the present generation of young people. This is the harvest of a terrible war too often overlooked.

It is also sometimes argued that the larger earning power of youth has contributed towards the teenage problem. This larger earning power is less evident now than a few years ago as the pattern of unemployment reappears in our economy. But, in so far as it does still exist, there is a strange element of truth in it. For young people who earn amounts approximating to adult earnings have a new sense of financial independence. But alongside this new sense go the old trammels of an

---

[22] Michael Argyle, *Psychology and Social Problems* (Methuen 1964).
[23] The ratio is about 8 boys to 1 girl.

adult-dominated society. So that we have the paradoxical position of young people, earning enough to be independent and yet confined by the traditions and rules of their society, to the domination of their parents. And this tends to sharpen the conflict between young and old. For the restrictions are felt as more irksome as financial independence is achieved. And with this goes an intensification of the differentiations between young and old. The teenagers adopt styles of dress, of forms of language and behaviour which mark them off from the adult world. This, of course, has always been a tendency but it seems to have reached striking proportions today so that the ways of the teenager constitute a sub-culture of its own.

The tragedy of youth today is that it has little positive sense of revolt. It can express its resentment of adult domination in a variety of ways that involve no decisive challenge. It can scandalise the adult world with its free and easy morals, shock it with its bizarre clothing and strident music. But nothing changes; for these things dissipate the energy of revolt.

This is a picture which, perhaps, can be exaggerated. For there are signs of a more positive direction to the revolt of youth. One may disagree with the objectives of the Campaign for Nuclear Disarmament and yet welcome its support among young people as a symptom of a search for more positive expressions of revolt. Paradoxically, that a movement that must unavoidably formulate its aims in a rather negative way can attract the support of many young people underlines this groping for positive expression. Among the young intellectuals, the writers, artists, actors, revolt, at the moment, takes the form of savagely satirising our most respected institutions and personalities.

How do Freudian and Marxist theories help us to understand the situation of modern youth? Freudian theory stresses the importance of stability in family relations. It points to the stresses and rivalries, the emotional complexities of inter-family relationships, that provide the soil for adult-adolescent

conflict. The adolescent seeks among its age-mates for the re-
assurance and security he does not find in his family. He
derives a status and identity, a sense of belonging that the
family and society in general have failed to provide.

Of Marxist theory we can say that it calls attention to the
interlocking of family and social structure. In capitalist
society economic insecurity is a constant factor for many
families. Inevitably, there will be a tendency for parents to
regard children as additional burdens on the finances of the
home, as extra mouths to feed. The values of a society that
measures success in monetary terms and applauds individual,
as opposed to co-operative, efforts, are bound to have a
corrupting influence in the family circle. At the very least, we
can say that such a society does not provide a favourable environment for the promotion of understanding between
young and old, that the conflicts within society tend to
exacerbate the conflicts within the family.

Ideally, we should seek to devise some means of encompass-
ing a smoother transition from childhood to adulthood, in
which the needs of the growing adolescent are sympathetic-
ally met. We should seek to devise more adequate prepara-
tion for the tasks of adulthood, introducing the young people
gradually but continuously to responsibilities. We should try
to show young people that we are on their side all the time.
But this enlightened attitude would require, I think, a whole
revolution in educational and social outlook, a break with the
values that rule today.

Our survey of Freudian and Marxist theory draws to an
end. We have seen that these two major intellectual forces of
our time provide important correctives for each other. Freudian theory makes us aware of the complexity of the subjective life but tends to look at it in isolation from the social
background. Marxism calls attention to the social determinants of human behaviour but tends to ignore the subjective pressures that lead men to enter into active relation-

ship with the social environment. Without the insights of Freudian theory, Marxism tends to be brutal and clumsy in its approach. No better example of this can be given than the Stalin era in the Soviet Union. Only a lack of psychological insight into the qualities that may impel a man to seek to dominate a party, particularly a revolutionary one, can explain how Stalin managed to hold power in his hands for so long. This was the point I stressed in my earlier efforts to get Marxists to think in Freudian terms.[24] I argued that Marxism, with its stress on revolutionary action, however valid this might be in particular historical circumstances, could become a rationalisation, masking the brutal compulsions of a sadistic mind. Their lack of psychological insight left Marxists unprepared for the developments of the Stalin leadership. They were hypnotised by this concept of the social determination of leadership – the leader as reflecting objective social forces. They saw people only in terms of class and social conditioning. Hence they left out of account the subtleties and variations of human psychology. That this or that individual might bring to his Marxist thinking a ruthless, toughminded, even sadistic, quality, did not seem to occur to them. The affirmation on his part of class consciousness was the important thing. Thus a leading British Marxist, Professor J. D. Bernal, in his review of *Freud and Marx*, wrote: 'Individuals are important, but only in so far as they crystallise in definite actions the determination of the party and class ... It is only necessary to compare a speech of Stalin's with one of Hitler's to see what a vast gulf divides the two conceptions of leadership.'[25]

[24] R. Osborn, *The Psychology of Reaction* (Gollancz 1938).

[25] J. D. Bernal, 'Psycho-Analysis and Marxism' (*Labour Monthly* 1937). Professor Bernal is too honest a scientist not to acknowledge the importance of the contributions of psycho-analysis but he seemed unable, at that time, to shake himself free from the official attitude of distrust concerning them. And this led him into an odd contradiction in which he seemed to be saying that Freudian theory is not so important because its influence is declining but, none the less is dangerous, because its influence is spreading. Thus he opens his review with the words: 'In recent years the Freudian wave has begun to recede.' And closes with: 'Freudian influence is an objective fact and is spreading slowly out from the bourgeois circles where it originated.'

True the conceptions of leadership were different but were the leaders themselves all that different psychologically? To judge from contemporary Soviet views on Stalin the answer is 'No'.

Stalin, no doubt, reflected, in many ways, the determination of the Russian workers and peasants and was able to give drive and direction to their struggles. But a Marxist, ready to learn from Freud, would have been alive to the dangers of a revolutionary leader bringing to the struggles of the workers a violence, ruthlessness and brutality more expressive of inner sadistic compulsions than the legitimate needs of the struggle.

It is not enough to evaluate the objective factors influencing men's decisions, especially those in leading positions. Men are moved by motives of love and hate, by factors in their personal histories, obscure yet compelling, that defy reduction to a crude social behaviourism. It is this that Marxists must learn. They would certainly be hard pressed to explain the bitter conflicts being waged among world Marxist leaders today, in terms only of objective social factors. Never have they needed the insights of Freud more.

Nevertheless, Marxism still has much to give in its vigorous criticism of the social irrationalities and injustices of our time. But it must enrich and humanise this criticism. It must draw upon the insights of Freudian theory if it is to escape the dogmatism that has made Marxism appear as a narrow and intolerant creed, ruled by a crude social behaviourism and unresponsive to the variety of individual differences among men and women.

Index

"His pages are impassioned, and yet dispassionate; polemical and yet impersonal; acute and yet wise.... His achievement is not, indeed, to have answered the question of the relationship of Marxism to psychoanalytic theory. That enormous task will require the sustained efforts of many thinkers. No, what Mr. Osborn has done is to ask that question: and to ask it in so intelligent, fruitful, and well-instructed a way that no one who cares for the development of Marxism as a living science will in future be able to neglect it."

—From the Introduction by John Strachey

TABLE OF CONTENTS

Dell Publishing Co., Inc. / Printed in U.S.A.